The Pakistan-Afghan Borderland:
Pashtun Tribes Descending into Extremism

The Pakistan-Afghan Borderland:
Pashtun Tribes Descending into Extremism
A Case Study of a Pashtun Tribe

By:
Khan Idris, PhD

Tribal Analysis Publishing
Richardson, Texas

The Pakistan-Afghan Borderland: Pashtun Tribes Descending into Extremism is published by Tribal Analysis Publishing of Richardson, Texas, in association with the Tribal Analysis Center of Williamsburg, Virginia.

Cover design by Robert Keene
Layout assistance by Jason Patti

The views and opinions expressed in this book are that of the author and do not necessarily represent those of his current or previous employers.

The Pakistan-Afghan Borderland: Pashtun Tribes Descending Into Extremism
First Edition
Library of Congress Cataloging-in-Publication Data
Idris, Khan. The Pakistan-Afghan Borderland: Pashtun Tribes Descending Into Extremism. 1. Pushtuns – Politics and government. | 2. Pushtuns – History. | 3. Salafiyah. | 4. Islamic fundamentalism. | I. Title.
ISBN 978-0-9819822-8-1
Library of Congress Control Number 2013953445

Foreword

The longer you can look back, the farther you can look forward[1]
—Winston Churchill

The Pashtun ethnic group, arguably the world's largest tribe with a population over 50 million, inhabit the Afghanistan-Pakistan borderland where they have lived for centuries in semi-isolation and from which, over time, their culture has evolved through a nomadic status to sedentary villages. While international borders have slowed, if not halted, their separate forms of occupational nomadic lives that included both herding and trading, their "tribal mindsets," as described so well by Dr. Akbar Ahmed, as *nang* (nomadic— honor bound) and *qalang* (sedentary—settled tax payers) continue to have an impact on their culture as "under-arching," factors that are unseen and not understood by their neighbors -- or even the tribesman themselves. The sedentary Pashtuns have settled into predictable, orderly lives in towns and "settled areas" while the *nang* mindset tribesmen occupy villages and isolated compounds from which they remain "warriors" with a responsibility for the defense of their extended families in the pursuit of what is defined for each adult male as an honorable life in his own eyes. This is done according to an ancient honor code that is understood best as *"Nangwali"* (honor bound) rather than the *"Pashtunwali"* that is so more commonly referred to and just as quickly misunderstood.

This "under-arching" cultural foundation requirement of

---

[1] In *Churchill by Himself* (2008), Appendix I: Red Herrings, ed. Langworth, Public Affairs, p. 577.

all Pashtun males having a *nang* mind-set is constantly present regardless of the religion they adopt -- and they have been shamanistic, and Zoroastrian. The late Ghani Khan suggests that they were also Buddhists who produced Buddhas having Pashtun faces before being converted to Islam by Qadiri and Naqshbandi missionaries. According to Sir Olaf Caroe, they resisted any forcible conversion to Islam and continued to resist invading Arab armies in eastern Afghanistan and Kabul where they remained unconverted as late as the year 850 of the Common Era.

Akbar Ahmed explains two very important factors regarding the Pashtuns retaining a nomadic mindset in his excellent study, "Pakhtun Economy and Society." First, he states a critical factor that needs to be understood by everyone studying these tribes: "Pakhtuns in *nang* areas have never been conquered and are aware that they have humbled the armies of two of the greatest empires known in India, the Mughal and the British."[2]

Second, and of an equal importance, these people have also been intractable problems for their notional rulers. Ahmed describes this very well:

"*Nang* Pashtuns reconcile with difficulty .... Even for a Pashtun king the *nang* tribesman is a formidable subject to dominate and equivalent versions of the immortal *Cri*

---

[2] This explained in chapter 5 of Akbar Ahmad's book, *Millennium and Charisma Among Pathans: A Critical Essay in Social Anthropology*, London: Routledge, 1976. This begins on pg. 76.

de Coeur[3] of 1879 of Yaqub Khan, king of Afghanistan. As he confronted the tribes gathering in Kabul to topple him, must have passed through the minds of many a ruler of Pakhtuns…. History is rooted in the *nang* Pakhtun's social consciousness…. Indeed, it is the last free place on earth."[4]

Other leaders in Pashtun areas have felt similar pressure from the *nang* tribes. Aminullah and his queen, Saroya, were forced to abdicate in recent history when tribes rebelled against their modernization efforts and the Soviets were opposed militarily by large numbers of tribesmen with a similar mindset following the communist coup that deposed -- and murdered – Muhammad Daoud Khan, the last Durrani ruler in Kabul before the current series of conflicts. The Taliban Movement and the current insurgency are composed primarily of *nang* Pashtuns intending to depose Hamid Karzai, a sedentary Popalzai Pashtun allied with outsiders.

Honor and tendencies toward violence are deeply rooted within the *nang* Pashtun and these "under-arching," basic cultural factors have a general code that is essentially defined differently, according to the region, with separately-weighted factors that are easily memorized by outsiders grasping at them, much like the proverbial drowning man and the straw, for understanding of this complex society. Unfortunately, the Code is redefined according to the specific portion of the population choosing to define it for themselves.

---

[3] As I understand it, this is a passionate, heart-felt outcry.
[4] This quote is located on page 93 of Ahmed's excellent study.

Pashtunwali is likely accepted in its entirety by the sedentary Pashtuns, but it is probably viewed in entirely different terms in Afghanistan's Helmand Province and in Pakistan's South Waziristan Agency, where Akbar Ahmed, in his anthropologist role, once served as Political Agent for Pakistan's government where *"Nangwali"* and its strict requirements for maintaining personal honor generally trump any of the other factors found within the larger Pashtunwali. From Ahmed:

> "Once he has identified the landmarks on his social landscape (*badal, melmastia, nanawatee, tor*) he can maneuver and manipulate other large unspoken areas.
>
> The democracy the Code implies is in a sense, real. No Pakhtun is the master of another. He is not bound by tedious daily ritual or commensally rules that can defile him. He interprets for action the fundamental requirements of the Code and the larger ones for Islam, often reduced to formal prayers, and apart from these is largely free to organize his life for himself.... Society may not approve but it will not act against him as long as he does not violate the Code. He alone is responsible for the laws of revenge. There is no concept of a group or lineage collectivity responsible for injury or death.... In *tor* or *badal* ceases, the father, husband, or son are individually responsible for implementing or seeking revenge."[5]

---

[5] Additional information regarding the individual Pashtun and his Code.

For the *nang* Pashtun, these responsibilities are constant requirements in a serious approach to demonstrating personal honor and "[a]part from the bloody demands of *tarboorwali*[6] and *tor*[7], a Pakhtun is defined by dignity and decorum in his affairs whether in public or private."[8] These often cryptic factors have remained as an absolute among the *nang* Pashtuns for thousands of years and are retained deeply within the cultural psychology of rural Pashtuns -- those who are now populating the ranks of the individual, loosely allied Taliban groups.

While the *nang* Pashtun clings tenaciously to the tenets associated with the more violent aspects of the Code, *badal, tarboorwali,* and *tor,* he is far more flexible in how he allows Islam to be defined for him. The excellent work done by anthropologist Louis Dupree explains a great deal of the reasons for the loose interpretations of Islam among the Pashtuns:

> "*The Islam practiced in Afghan villages, nomad camps, and most urban areas would be almost unrecognizable to a sophisticated Muslim scholar. Aside from faith in Allah and in Mohammad as the Messenger of Allah, most beliefs relate to localized, pre-Muslim customs. Some of the ideals of Afghan tribal society run counter to Islamic principles. The Pashtunwali (traditional code of the Pashtun hills), for example, demands blood vengeance, even on fellow Muslims, contradicting Sura 4:92-93: "If is not for a believer to*

---

[6] Cousin enmity normally found between paternal cousins having an equal claim to the paternal grandfather's inheritance.

[7] This term is related to any aspects of honor impacting women.

[8] Ahmed, pg. 96.

*kill a believer unless it be by mistake. He who hath killed
a believer by mistake must free a believing slave, and pay
the blood-money to the family of the slain, unless they
remit it as a charity.[9]"*

Dupree explains further:

*The traditionalists feed fuel to the peasant-tribal
beliefs in predestination; aided and abetted by religious
leaders at every level. Those at the bottom of the
hierarchy, the village mullah, are often non-literate
farmers who often function as part-time religious leaders.
Technically, Islam has no organized clergy, and every
man can be a mullah. Anyone can lead in prayer.... Thus
the essentially non-Islamic belief of the non-literate
Muslim that Allah planned all in advance excuses
tyranny, and prepares man to accept whatever fate hands
to them.[10]*

As a result, the overarching social influence of Islam
tends to shift quickly. While still believing in Allah and his
Messenger, Muhammad, different groups of Pashtuns have been
Hanafi Muslims, Sufis, Roshanis[11], Ismailis, Shi'a, and Salafist
Wahabbis, often following different schools of thought within
the same tribes. Some tribes, especially those that tend to be
most superstitious and turn quickly to their mullahs for
explanations of events that are not easily understood, were called

---

[9] Dupree sources this quote to Pickthall, 1954, pg. 88; Dupree, pg. 105.
[10] Dupree, pp. 107-108.
[11] Pir Roshan created the Pashtun alphabet and preached about women's
rights.

"priest-ridden" by the British and these Pashtuns seem to be among the most easily persuaded to adopt a new approach to the practice of Islam.

In Pakistan's northwestern region, they appear to be gravitating toward a restricted, extremist form of Islamic orientation, Salafism, which provides a favorable religious, social, and political space for more militant groups, including Al-Qa'ida, Lashkar-e Taiba, and the Pakistani Taliban groups. While people wonder how extremist leaders, such as Osama Bin Laden and Ayman al-Zawahiri could find a safe havens in the Pashtun-dominated areas, this combination of rugged physical terrain combined with an equally rugged social, political, and religious environment explains why militants are able to find a safe haven within Pashtun-controlled areas. The reasons seem to lay in a gradual, but a persistent religious shift from the relatively more tolerant Hanafi Sufi beliefs to more the restricted and militant Hanbali Salafi interpretation of Islam that is more commonly practiced in the Middle East instead of South Asia. While it is true that the Pashtuns are a unique race with a peculiar way of life governed by varying degrees of Pashtunwali that attracts militants into their "clusters," a key explanation of Pashtun tribes' militancy and the ease with which militant groups emerge, seems to involve a relatively swift religious evolution from their traditional Sufism to the new, nearly alien Salafism. This new religious orientation, sometimes mixed with local cultural and social dynamics, is generally blamed for the Pashtun tribes tolerating, and in some instances encouraging, the militants' activities in the border area and beyond.

These same Pashtun tribes rebelled against British colonial power in the latter part of 19th century, fought against the Soviet occupation of Afghanistan in 1980s, and have been fighting against Pakistan's and Afghanistan's governments. This study will explain the process of the Pashtun tribes' gradual shifting of religious views along with explanations why these tribes have revolted periodically against different governments. Understanding the Pashtun tribes' religious orientation helps explain why Salafist militant groups find safety in Pashtun-inhabited areas. This shifting of religious orientation helps explain factors that drive a Pashtun toward certain behaviors and motivates them to action, either to extend support to the militants or withdraw support from these same extremists. Understanding the shifting religious orientation of Pashtuns' processes related to changes helps to explain instincts of the Pashtuns and may help with ending the militancy and extremism in Pakistan and Afghanistan. Winston Churchill observed during the British expedition against one of several Pashtun rebellions led by local Mullahs:

> *"I have been told that if a white man could grasp it fully, and were to understand their mental impulse—if he knew, when it was their honour to stand by him, and when it was their honour to betray him; when they were bound to protect and when to kill him—he might, by judging his times and opportunities, pass safely from one end of the mountains to the other."[12]*

In this major study of Pashtun tribal hybridization shifting toward Salafism Islam, Dr. Idris argues that central to the understanding of the current militancy and extremism in

---

[12] See Churchill's *The Story of the Malakand Field Force*, pg. 20.

Pakistan and Afghanistan is the recognition of the methods utilized as the Salafists made inroads into Pashtun society along with the impact of Salafists on the tribal, social, political, religious, cultural, and even the daily lives of the Pashtuns. This study utilizes a series of case studies from a small village in the Pashtun border region to demonstrate that the Pashtun tribes in the Pakistan-Afghanistan borderland are in the process of shifting toward Salafism as their traditional Hanafi Sufism beliefs are discarded. The author argues that this shift has been undermining the traditional tribal and religious structure to create much of the instability that fuels conflict in the region.

As discovered in the observations that resulted from these case studies, Salafists have been successful because they fully understand the local Pashtun layered society, with each layer having its own dynamics, a separate leadership structure, different complex decision-making processes, and its own mechanism for generating or ending conflict. The study revealed that Salafists began to target tribal elites to make them amirs (leaders) instead of focusing on the lower status mullahs as was done in previous conflicts and this study reveals that this new approach has been very effective in gaining access, if not actual control, within local Pashtun villages.

The study also found that Salafist recruitment of tribal elites has been accelerating the rate at which the Pashtun tribes are shifting toward Salafism. With the ability of the new amirs to spread their influence across tribal boundaries, they have been extremely effective in mediating local disputes, a key function once performed traditional tribal leaders who are being further marginalized, while also showing that these Salafist amirs also sidelined traditional religious leaders, who are gradually viewed as "disco mullahs" or "corrupt mullahs" by local Pashtuns coming under Salafist influence. These Salafist amirs also have been instrumental in uniting tribes by using Islam as a rallying "chiga," a commonly used means of uniting tribes to a single cause, and raise tribal lashkars, a tribal war party, against a real or perceived invasion or threat from "infidels, a potential occupation by an "un-Islamic" regime, or to oppose local warlords who resist the emerging Salafist authority. These young Salafist amirs also have been using their positions to provide social services, such as conflict resolution, religious guidance, legal authority, etc., for local Pashtun tribes to further erode both the power and influence of the traditional tribal leaders and religious clerics.

This study contains very useful material that provides a unique insight about Salafist methods used to insert control over local Pashtun communities that used to result in a cycle in which the traditional tribal leaders generally regained control of their tribes. Shifting the focus from attempting to gain control of the more superstitious tribes through the lower status mullah class to the more elite families, the previously reversible cycle of the clerics against the tribe's secular leadership may have halted with Salafists gaining permanent control.

Dr. Idris accurately describes what is likely to be the initial phase of Tablighi Jamaat's infiltration into the daily lives of Pashtun villagers in what is likely to be the first of several stages. Even a causal look at the basic data associated with the subtle shifting leaves observers wondering about what will emerge in future phases of Tablighi Jamaat. Violent amirs, such as Hakimullah Mahsud and the recently deceased Mullah Nazir, now lead equally violent insurgent groups opposed to the United States in Afghanistan and at home in Pakistan. These individuals, and others of the same ilk, seem to come from the lower classes of Pashtun tribes, not unlike the mullah class of the past that led earlier rebellions and it is very probable that these men simply hijacked the "amir" title and the legitimacy any connection to Tablighi Jamaat might lend them. The other stages into which these new amirs who emerged from the upper, educated classes of Pashtuns may best understood if we follow Churchill's injunction that leads farther back into previous instability in the same area. Connections between "founding fathers" and links to political events tell a great deal that might be expected from Tablighi Jamaat when it reaches its internally projected full stride. The warnings are there.

The founder of the movement Mohammad Ilyas, had for his Pir, Rashid Ahmad Gangohi, one of the founders of the Deoband madrassa.[13] Both Deobandism and its lineal descendent, as it is best seen, Tablighi Jamaat, emerged during periods when Islam was under increasing stress. Deobandism's missionary program developed following the revolt against the British in India, the one they referred to as the "Great Mutiny," and Mohammad Ilyas developed a very similar missionary program in the region south of New Delhi where Muslims were converting to Hinduism in 1927. This second great reformist movement didn't develop in political isolation, either. Mohammad Ilyas was studying at Deoband at a time when the

---

[13] Gaborieau, Marc, "What is Left of Sufism in Tablighi Jama'at?" *Archives de Sciences Sociales des Religions*, Vol. 51, (2006), pg. 57.

Indian nationalist movement was gaining momentum, the Ottoman Empire collapsed along with the Muslim Caliphate, the Muslim Brotherhood emerged in Egypt, and Abdul Ala Maududi's initial writings on jihad that initiated the first stages of Muslim fundamentalism appeared in 1927, the year Ilyas founded Tablighi Jamaat.[14] While the movement claims to be non-violent and apolitical, they attract political leaders, such as Nawaz Sharif, Farooq Leghari, and Zia ul-Haq, the essentially fundamentalist prime minister of Pakistan who was responsible for the arrival of Salafists into the country during the anti-Soviet jihad of the 1980's.

At the same time, Tablighi Jamaat appears to be engaged in a quiet conflict with the adherents of Sufism in the region, much like Deobandis are involved, who condemn most of Sufism's mystical practices even though the Deobandis are a hybridization of several Sufi orders, themselves. The al-Tabligh movement is best viewed as a "hybridization-in-process" emerging from Deobandism. Their missionaries are appearing worldwide where they move door-to-door, and are called "Muslim Jehovah's Witnesses" as they quietly challenge other Muslims about what they would say during the "End Days." Visits to mosques result in lectures about "jihad being an internal war" as additional individuals are drawn into the "apolitical movement."

Marc Gaborieau provides us with a valuable Churchillian reminder: "So the climate in which the Tabligh movement was born was not at all one of pacifism, nor even of purely defensive

---

[14] Ibid, pg. 60.

Jihad; in the milieu of Muhammad Ilyas, holy war with the sword was considered an essential duty of Islam." [15]

Dr. Idris has provided us with an excellent view of the processes utilized within the initial phase of al-Tablighi operations, but there is a clearly distinct likelihood that there are more stages of this Muslim reform movement yet to be seen.

– Tribal Analysis Center

---

[15] Gaborieu, op. cit. pg. 60.

Preface and Acknowledgements

This book is a follow up to my previous two books: *Jirgas: Pashtun Participatory Governance*, and *Jirgas: The Pashtun Way of Conflict Resolution*. It explains the reasons and mechanisms that caused the Pashtuns along the border separating Pakistan and Afghanistan,* to begin to accept Salafism during recent years. The principal tenet of Salafism is that the form of Islam preached by Prophet Muhammad and practiced by his Companions, as well as the second and third generations succeeding them, was pure, unadulterated, and therefore the ultimate authority for the interpretation of the two sources of revelation given to Muhammad, namely the Qur'an and the Sunnah.[16, 17, 18, 19]

This study is the first in-depth, micro-level study of the Pashtun tribes' shifting religious orientation within a Sunni religious ideology that is followed by different political groups in the region, including the Taliban and Al-Qa'ida. These Pashtun tribes inhabit southern and eastern Afghanistan and the northwestern region of Pakistan where in recent years, Al-Qa'ida, Pakistan's Taliban known as Tehriq-e-Taliban Pakistan (TTP), the Afghan Taliban, and other militants have found safe haven. From these safe havens, these groups have been waging a

---

[16] Moosa, Ebrahim, *"Ghazali And The Poetics Of Imagination"*, p. 21
[17] Baker, Dr Abdul-Haqq, *"Extremists in Our Midst: Confronting Terror"*, Palgrave Macmillan, 2011
[18] Meijer, Roel (2009). "Introduction". In Meijer, Roel. *Global Salafism: Islam's New Religious Movement*. Columbia University Press, p. 34
[19] *"Jihad" By Gilles Kepel, Anthony F. Roberts*. Books.google.com. 2006-02-24.http://books.google.com/?id=OLvTNk75hUoC&dq=islamism&prints ec=frontcover. Retrieved 2010-04-18

xxi

violent insurgency both in Pakistan and Afghanistan while posing a threat to the region, the United States, and the remainder of the West.

This study reveals my own personal views about how Pakistan's indigenous Salafist movement, the Tablighi Jamaat, has made inroads into the local Pashtun tribes, and the consequences of this not only for the tribes, but also for regional stability, and the global war on terrorism. I will describe how Pashtuns live, their religious and tribal traditions; identify the drivers of this shift toward Salafism, and the possible consequences of this change to a new religious orientation.

As the world's attention is fixed on the Pashtun area along the Pakistan-Afghanistan borderland where terrorism has become a huge criminal enterprise, it is extremely important to understand the inner workings of the people and their religious practices. By understanding their religious practices and the internal dynamics of the local inhabitants, intellectuals and their students will be able to understand why some Pashtuns participate in terrorist activities and why some Pashtuns harbor non-Pashtun religious extremists. This knowledge will help understand why some tribes gravitate toward extremism while others do not.

I'd like to thank my late father Hajji Yunus Khan, who passed away in May 2010, whose love motivated me to travel to the village every year. Without these visits, this study would not have been possible. During my stays in the village, I engaged my father in discussions, which helped generate the ideas contained in this book. I also would like to thank my family, especially my wife Marina, daughter Chezmeen, and son Behram for unconditional support and love during my numerous trips to

Pakistan and during the writing of this manuscript. Without their love and support, I could not have completed this challenging task. I would also like to extend my thanks to my own tribesmen, the Jehangir Khel, who gave me their full support every time I lived among them. Their hospitality provided opportunities to observe events without relying upon secondary sources.

I further thank my friends, both in the United States and in Pakistan, who gave me assistance each time I visited Pakistan. They were hospitable enough to provide me food and lodging in their homes. I am particularly indebted to my friend Dr. Abdul Samad Wazir, a doctor and scion of a prominent Waziri family, for giving me full support during my trips into the region. I would also like to thank my friend, Nawabzada Jehangir Saeed Khan, and his brother, Nawab Salahuddin Saeed Khan, grandsons of the former rulers of Chitral and Amb states in northwest of Pakistan, for their hospitality. My thanks also go to my friend Arbab Amin-ul Hasanat, a member of a prominent Arbab family of Tehkal Bala near Peshawar, for his generosity during my trips to Pakistan. In addition to these friends, numerous peasants, tribesmen, relatives, and friends deserve special thanks for extending their hospitality to make this project a success.

Finally, I would like to thank all those people both in and outside the region who have been working hard to bring peace and prosperity to the great Pashtun people. Pashtuns have been the victims of external politics for centuries. Let us hope that one day this will end with peace and prosperity for the Pashtun people.

Prologue

In April 1993, as an aspiring writer and academic, I left cold, breezy and urban Champaign, Illinois, after successfully completing a doctorate program at the University of Illinois. After traveling about 24 hours, I arrived in Islamabad at 5 AM on a British Airline flight from London's Heathrow airport. My brother and nephews were there to pick me up and after I collected my luggage and walked out of customs, I saw my brother Akhtar and my two nephews, Bilal and Shahid, who were excited to greet me after an absence of over four years. From the airport, I was taken to my ancestral village Pak Kaya, located in the heart of Swabi district of the Northwest Frontier Province, commonly referred to as NWFP, but now renamed Khyber Pakhtunkhwa.

At the time, I was young, energetic, and full of new ideas. Being a student of social change in tribal societies, especially the Pashtuns, I knew the area was rich with opportunity for testing ideas I learned in my graduate programs. On the way to the village, we stopped at a restaurant during morning prayers. My younger brother and two school-age nephews were with me in the car. When we made a right turn from main highway to the local road into a town locally known as Anbar, we saw a young man with a black turban. I looked at the man, but I did not recognize him. The man's clothing was unique, his beard was long, the turban was unusual, and his style of walking was not local.

"Who is this man?" I asked.

My brother responded, "Your friend, Fiaz Khan, don't you recognize him?"

"What happened to him?" I asked.

"Oh, he became Tablighi?" Tablighi Jamaat is one of the Salafist proselytization organizations in the region.

"But he was a whisky drinker and very secular," I noted.

"Recently he and Jamil's son became Tablighi," my brother responded.

This was my first contact with Salafism. After two hours journey from the airport, we arrived at the village at dawn where we could hear the sound of "Zakir", a Sufi ritual that occurs after morning prayers. The next day was Friday and I slept the whole morning but awakened at 1:00 PM and went to the village mosque for Friday prayers where I observed a group of Tablighi Jamaat members in the main mosque. They were huddled together in the corner and I did not see any locals in the group.

I asked a tribesman, "Who are these men?"

"Oh, they are Tablighi. Your friend Fiaz Khan is there, too. They are just wasting time here," the villager observed.

I just ignored my former friend, Fiaz Khan, and his group and went home after prayers.

On the following Monday, I reported to the NWFP Agriculture University (now renamed Khyber Pakhtunkhwa Agriculture University) where I was appointed an adviser to the Vice Chancellor. In my previous years as a political science student, and a member of the Pashtun Students Federation, a secular, nationalist student organization in early 1970's and 1980's in Peshawar University, there were few Tablighi Jamaat members in the area and the entire organization was new to the region.

The more commonly encountered Jamaat-i-Islami student wing known as Islami Jamiat-e-Tulba (JT) gained a foothold on the Peshawar University campus in 1980s because JT was receiving financial support from Hezb-i-Islami (HI) of Afghanistan, that was headquarted in Peshawar. Hezb-i-Islami was one of the seven anti-Soviet Mujahideen groups fighting in Afghanistan. The area's colleges and universities were generally dominated by secular, nationalist, or socialist groups, including the Pakistan People's Party and its affiliated People's Students Federation and the Awami National Party with its Pashtun Students Federation. The use of music, concerts, films - even English language films - at movie theaters, the use of hashish, and even occasional alcohol use was common among the students. I observed few bearded students on campus with some students from JT observed to have short beards, but the rest of the student body was generally secular. Except for Friday prayers, most of the students would not even pray regularly.

Every weekend I would visit my village where the inhabitants were uniformly Sufi. There was not a single member of Tablighi Jamaat in the village, but on campus I met a librarian named Shakirrullah. I called him "Pir Saib" out of respect because he was a very religious, decent man. Interestingly, he was a member of a Tablighi Jamaat, but was not an Amir, a leadership position in the organization. Shakirullah would preach Islam and would ask me to pray. Out of respect, I would listen to his advice, but did not necessarily follow it. There was another Tablighi Jamaat member named Gul Rose who was a clerk at the university. By 1993, professors dressed as Tablighi

Jamaat had begun to make inroads into the teaching faculty at the campus.

By 1993, the Tablighi Jamaat dominated the entire campus. During an annual gathering in November every year for the Tablighi Jamaat's Ijtama in Lahore, the whole campus was shut down. I observed several buses leaving in November 1993 for a three-day pilgrimage – their ijtama – the annual gathering in Lahore. In 1993, I could feel their presence on the campus as I observed changes in Peshawar University and there were several active Tablighi Jamaat members among the senior teaching faculty.

Jamaat-i-Islami's student wing, Islami Jamiat-e-Tulba, became very assertive and I observed frequent violence between Islami Jamiat-e-Tulba and the secular student organization. In one instance in 1983 Islami Jamiat-e-Tulba members killed a leader of the People's Students Federation at Khyber Medical College. In aftermath of the killing, the campus was closed to prevent revenge killing. Everyone on campus knew that a senior member of Islami Jamiat-e-Tulba from Hazara region killed the medical student and People's Students Federation vowed to take revenge, but the Islami Jamiat-e-Tulba, which was backed by Hitz-e-Islami, one of the Mujahideen groups that was supported by Pakistani government, was very strong. Despite this killing and the fact that Islami Jamiat-e-Tulba was backed by Hitz-e-Islami, the secular students' organizations were strong. In the student body elections in the university and the departments, the secular student organizations that included the Pakhtun Students Federation and People's Students Federation, would win the election. By 1996, one could see only Islami Jamiat-e-Tulba presence. The Tablighi Jamaat and Deoband affiliated Jamiat-ul-

Islam (JUI) student organization were hardly visible. Please note, the JI and Islami Jamiat-e-Tulba had been dominating the educational institutions in Punjab province in Pakistan since 1960s. However, Islami Jamiat-e-Tulba could not find a political space in Peshawar University because the secular students organizations were strong.

When I arrived on campus in 1993, the Tabligh Jamaat and JUI affiliated student organization's footprints were everywhere. These two groups were even challenging Islami Jamiat-e-Tulba on the campus. Please note, Jamaat-i-Islami and Islami Jamiat-e-Tulba are revivalist movements that believed in the revival of Sharia law and followed the Muslim Brotherhood in Middle East. In contrast, the Tablighi Jamaat (TJ) and JUI followed Salafist ideology. Both supported the ideology of the Taliban and Al-Qa'ida, if not their tactics.

By 1993, I saw that the secular activities on campus were banned. The movie theater built on campus by Agha Khan, a spiritual leader of the Ismaili sect of Islam, was shut down by the Islamists. Music concerts, which had been common on the campus, were banned and music in public was forbidden. There was a noticeable change in students' appearance. One could see more young men with beards on campus by late 1993 and the whole campus would shut down in November for the Tablighi Jamaat's Ijtama in Lahore.

During my visit to village, I saw frequent visits by Tablighi Jamaat. Despite this, I noticed that the village remained committed to Sufism. As the Tablighi Jamaat visits increased, I observed the Sufism followers practicing rituals including "Zakir" before and after the five daily prayers. In an apparent reaction to the aggressive behavior of Tablighi Jamaat, the Sufi supporters at the village were aggressive in practicing their religion. They were practicing more rituals than normal, including the Sufi's Zakir.

I left Pakistan in 1993 and came to the US; however, I continued to visit the village every year. During all these visits, and especially since the late 1990s, I witnessed a noticeable change as Tablighi Jamaat established a foothold in the village. As noted above, there was not a single Tablighi Jamaat member in the village in the mid-1990s, however by 2010, I observed that almost all the young men in the village were active members.

In March and then in May 2010, I visited the village. I stayed one month each time and began to document the change from Sufism to Salafism. Please note that I am not a scholar of Islam and the main purpose of this study is to explain the process of change in the village. It does not take sides or argue in favor of either Sufism or Salafism. Being a student of social change, I will attempt to analyze and document this important social change from Sufism to Salafism in Pak Kaya.

This study also focuses on Pashtun tribes, and in it I have attempted to describe tribal village life and to address the following questions: What were the religious practices prevalent among the Pashtun tribes especially in the village? Were they tolerant and secular in nature? Are Pashtun tribes sliding toward rigid Salafism and why? What is the future of these tribes as they gravitate toward Salafism? Are they going to be prone to the religious current championed by al-Qaida and its allies who are using violent means to bring a political change in the Muslim world and beyond? What will it mean for the stability and security of the Pashtun-inhabited areas in Pakistan and

Afghanistan? What does it mean for the stability of the regimes in Pakistan and Afghanistan?

I will show that in the past, Pashtun tribes were very tolerant in their practice of Islam. The tribes followed the Hanafi Sufi School of thought, which preached tolerance and accommodation. In their daily practice of religion, the Pashtun tribesmen would always show tolerance toward other religions. For example, there were a significant number of Sikhs and Hindus who lived among the Pashtuns. The Pashtun nationalist party Khudai Khadmat Gar (helpers on behalf of God) joined the All India Congress, a Hindu-dominated party in India, and opposed the creation of the Muslim homeland Pakistan in 1947. Many religious leaders would view some of the Islamic practices followed by the Pashtun tribesmen as un-Islamic or perhaps only borderline Islamic. Despite this, the Pashtuns continued to practice those rituals.

Since the 1980s, different religious groups have been fighting for control of the Pashtun tribal landscape of Pakistan and Afghanistan. From more radical elements affiliated with Al-Qa'ida and an assertive Jamaat-i-Islami, to a pacifist Tablighi Jamaat, all have found followers among the Pashtun tribesmen. This study reveals what is happening within one Pashtun tribe and why it is happening. Why are the local Pashtun tribesmen gravitating toward these new religious groups? What have been the effects of this shift from the old Sufi religious practices to the new Salafi practices? What are the social, cultural, and economic results of these changes? Are these changes manageable or are they generating tensions that may translate into a tribal civil war such has been occurring for years between the Sufi and Deobandi groups—Ansar-ul-Islam and Lashkar-i-

Islam—within the Afridi tribe in the Khyber Agency? What is the outlook for the region and is it possible to return to peace and prosperity?

This small tribe and village are ideal for a case study because there is a knowledge gap when it comes to micro-level analysis within the Pashtun area. Most of the studies analyze the local militant and religious phenomena at a very high level, with little focus on social and religious change at the village level. Since Pashtun tribes are fractured and decentralized, understanding the local tribal and village dynamics helps explain the phenomena of extremism, fundamentalism, militancy, jihad fervor, Al-Qa'ida's presence, the TTP and the Taliban insurgency in the area.

During research for two previous studies—*Jirga: Pashtun Participatory Governance* and *Jirgas: The Pashtun Way of Conflict Resolution*—I noticed that the village was gradually gravitating from Sufism to Salafism. This current study addresses the issues of leadership, decision-making and conflict resolution among the Pashtuns, as well as Pashtun tribes' descent into Salafism and the reasons for the change. This study is not about Sufism or Salafism, but it is a study about a Pashtun village and the reasons for the shift in its religious orientation.

TABLE OF CONTENTS

The Pakistan-Afghan Borderland: Pashtun Tribes Descending into Extremism

Introduction

The Pashtun tribes inhabiting the Pakistan-Afghanistan borderland have been gravitating toward Islamic Salafism since the 1990's. The principal tenet of Salafism is that the form of Islam preached by Prophet Muhammad and practiced by his Companions, as well as the second and third generations succeeding them, was pure, unadulterated, and, therefore, the ultimate authority for the interpretation of the two sources of revelation given to Muhammad, namely the Qur'an and the Sunnah. The Pashtun tribes' shifting from a traditional Sufi Sunni Islamic ideology to a new Salafi

Some Sunni Islamic belief has fueled militancy, intolerance, extremism, and sectarianism in the area, threatening regional and international stability. This transformation from Sufism to Salafism and the resulting instability and militancy has impacted the local Pashtun tribes the most. In addition, this transformation has been fueling violence in the region and beyond the Pashtun areas.

The old Sufi Sunni Islam was more tolerant and accommodative. The Pirs, the custodians of Sufism, would either tolerate or turn a blind eye toward some of the primitive tribal practices even though some of those practices were clearly un-Islamic in the eyes of the more rigid Salafists. In contrast, the followers of this new Salafism do not tolerate any ancient tribal practices which are seen as un-Islamic, causing resentment from the local Pashtuns, which has resulted in violence and intolerance in the region.

The Pirs and the Sufis coexisted with the traditional tribal leadership structure for centuries. Instead of challenging the traditional tribal leadership, the Pirs and the Sufis supported the local Khans and Maliks. Pirs, Sufis, and the traditional Pashtun leaders prevented any attempt by the firebrand Mullahs to take control of tribal society. In some instances, the Mullahs assumed control of the leadership when it was threatened by an external enemy, especially if the enemy was non-Muslim. However, once the threat receded, the Pirs and the local traditional leaders would quickly force the Mullahs to drop back to their traditional role in the society, performing religious services as a prayer leader.[20] During annual visits, I observed that in traditional Pashtun society, there was always equilibrium among the three competing forces—the Sufi Pirs, the Mullahs, and the Pashtun leaders. In the past, Pashtun leaders used the Sufi Pirs, who enjoyed religious respect among the tribesmen, to constrain the Mullahs. This allowed them to maintain the political and religious balance in the society and discipline the unpredictable Mullahs. The Sufi Pirs, who enjoyed religious capital, maintained a tenuous balance between the Mullahs' religious power and the traditional leaders' secular power. Traditional Pashtun leaders used the Sufi Pirs and their religious authority to contain the Mullahs' aspirations for power. Maintaining this balance among these three local leaders played an important role in keeping peace and tranquility in Pashtun society.

---

[20] Akbar S. Ahmed, *Resistance and Control in Pakistan.* Routledge, London, 2004

At times, Pashtun society experienced an imbalance in which the Mullahs enjoyed sweeping power, sidelining both the traditional Sufi Pirs and the tribal leaders and fueling conflict and violence. For example, between 1842 and 1897 the Mullahs mobilized the local tribes against the British colonial power in India. This resulted in a series of military campaigns against the British colonials, causing thousands of casualties. In the end, with the help of the British, the traditional Pashtun leaders managed to reclaim their leadership position, ending the conflict and violence. The local Sufi Pirs also regained their influence, neutralizing the negative influence of the Mullahs. [21]

Similarly, during the jihad against the Soviet occupation of Afghanistan, the Salafist Mullahs took control of the tribal leadership, marginalizing both the Sufi Pirs and the traditional Pashtun leaders. This resulted in an imbalance among the three aspirants to the leadership positions in the Pashtun society—the Sufi Pirs, the Mullahs and Pashtun leaders. The result of this disequilibrium was more violence. The Mullahs' power reached a peak when the Taliban took control of Afghanistan in the 1990s, totally sidelining the Sufi Pirs and the traditional tribal leaders. Between 2007 and 2010, the Salafists either killed or expelled the Pirs and the traditional Pashtun leaders in the Federally Administered Tribal Areas (FATA) of Pakistan and Swat district of Khyber-Pakhtunkhwa, fueling an insurgency against Islamabad. This disrupted relationship among the Pirs, the Mullahs, and the traditional tribal leaders remains along the

---

[21] For more detail, see *Frontier of Faith: Islam in the Indo-Afghan Borderland* by Sana Haroon, Columbia University Press, New York, 2007, and *The Story of the Malakand Field Force* by Winston S. Churchill, reprinted by Bibliobazaar, 2006.

Pakistan-Afghanistan borderland and it is argued in this study that as long as this disequilibrium exists in Pashtun society, there will be instability and violence.

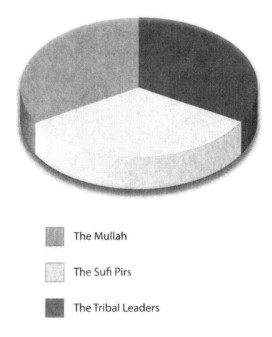

The Mullah

The Sufi Pirs

The Tribal Leaders

Figure 1. Societal Equilibrium When Power is Distributed Equally.

This study notes that modern Salafism in the region is a unique phenomenon and shows that the supporters and leaders of Salafism believe in the same ideology, but they are divided over the implementation strategy of this new ideology. Some Salafist groups use force as a mean to impose their ideology while others adopt a purely peaceful approach to preaching the new beliefs. They even view the use of force as un-Islamic. For example, the Taliban claim to follow the example of the Tablighi Jamaat, a group they describe as a peaceful proselytizing Salafist group,

4

but the Taliban does not follow the spirit of Tablighi Jamaat's approach when it comes to enforcing Salafism. In contrast, the Tablighi Jamaat does not approve of the Taliban's use of force to enforce Salafism. Despite these differences, all Salafi groups believe in the same Salafi ideology. They are against Sufism and the traditional tribal structure. In addition, both Salafi groups have been undermining the traditional axis of the Pirs and the traditional, more secular Pashtun leaders. The Taliban and their supporters from Al-Qa'ida have been even killing the local Pirs and the traditional tribal leaders. Especially in Pakistan's tribal areas where Al-Qa'ida and its allies are more commonly encountered, the Salafists have also been destroying Sufi shrines, which have been a major source of the Pirs' financial and social power in the Pashtun society. For example, I visited the Pir Baba shrine in Buner in early 1980s and observed visiting disciples throwing money at the shrine. In the evening, the custodians of the shrines were seen collecting the money. I also observed Ali Pur Pir, Jala Bajee Pir and Jilbai Pir, three Pirs that are discussed later in the study, collecting money from the villagers.

It is not as worrisome that the local Pashtun tribesmen are turning toward this new brand of Islam and becoming more religious, but the fact that some tribesmen use force to impose their ideology on the others is frightening. In addition, this group utilizes Salafism to challenge the state's writ in both Pakistan and Afghanistan. The local tribesmen have also been using Salafism to destroy the local tribal and religious structure as low status Pashtuns are enabled to take control of entire tribal regions in what is best described as a landless peasant revolt as the actual owners, the khans, are displaced. Furthermore, the Pashtun Salafists use Salafism as a cover to invite Al-Qa'ida and

5

other militant Islamic groups into their mix, threatening regional and global security and stability as militant extremists from Central Asia and Al-Qa'ida who relocated into Taliban-controlled areas of Afghanistan continue to plan and implement terrorist operations from safe havens inside Pakistan's Pashtun regions. Once Salafists empowered with new ideology, a highly motivated membership and material resources brought in by the non-Pashtun militants, the local Pashtuns are able to challenge the traditional tribal and religious leadership and they use their newly gained power to destroy the existing tribal and religious controls. As these are damaged and broken, chaos is likely to produce a power vacuum that may be quickly filled by the more radical elements such as the Taliban and Al-Qa'ida.

Salafism: A Unique Phenomenon for Pakistan

This study shows that the phenomenon of the Salafism among the Pashtuns is unique because the current insurgency and the Salafist movement are not led by the Mullahs. The current movement is dominated by tribesmen who enjoy both religious and tribal legitimacy. The Amirs of Tablighi Jamaat, the Salafi leaders, enjoy both religious and tribal respect. In the past, the tribal leaders would have had tribal capital and the Mullahs would have had religious capital. If required, the Mullahs would utilize tribal capital to wage jihad against an external enemy. However, the Mullahs could not sustain control over both tribal and religious elements for long. Eventually, the tribal capital would gravitate back to the legitimate tribal leaders, creating an atmosphere of peace.

In traditional Pashtun society, the religious capital was historically divided between the Mullahs and the Sufi Pirs and the Mullahs' religious capital was shared by the Sufi Pirs. This would tip the balance of power in favor of local tribal leaders and would also constrain the Mullahs' behavior and actions. The Sufi Pirs who were supporters of the traditional tribal elders avoided aligning themselves with the Mullahs.

Current Salafism in Pakistan and Afghanistan is different because the Amirs, the leaders of the Salafism, enjoy both religious and tribal power. For example, Hafiz Gul Bahadar , in North Waziristan Agency, is both a legitimate tribal leader and a religious leader. However, he is not a Mullah and did not have any formal religious education. His first name, Hafiz, suggests that he memorized the Koran, giving him notional religious credentials within society. Gul Bahadar is not a prayer leader in any community in North Waziristan, however he extends all the services a traditional Pashtun leader is expected to provide. For example, Gul Bahadar calls the jirgas, heads those jirgas, mediates disputes, and provides security for the weak. Since he is a local Tablighi Jamaat Amir, he is also perceived as a religious man, both by local Mullahs, and his own tribesmen.

Mangal Bagh, who is a Sepha tribesman, a clan of the Afridi Pashtun tribe, and a leader of Deobandi Taliban known as Lashkar-i-Islam in Khyber Agency, is not a Mullah but like Gul Bahadur, enjoys both tribal and religious legitimacy. The late Commander Nazir in South Waziristan Agency was a tribesman from Kaka Khel, a clan of the Zili Khel Ahmadzai Wazir tribe, but he was also a Tablighi Jamaat Amir who dominated the area, which gave him both tribal and religious legitimacy. Abdul Wali (also known as Omar Khalid) in Mohmand Agency is a Safi

7

tribesman as well as a Tablighi Amir. Like the others, Abdul Wali enjoys both tribal and religious credentials. Faqir Mohammad, the leader of Tehrik-I Taliban in Bajaur, is a local Mahmund tribesman as well as a Tablighi Jamaat Amir, also enjoying both tribal and religious authority. Even in Afghanistan, Mullah Barader and Mullah Omar are not Mullahs in the traditional Pashtun sense. Omar is a Hotak Ghilzai and Barader is Popalzai Durrani. They are legitimate tribal members who have legitimate tribal roles.

The Taliban are powerful due to the fact that they enjoy both tribal recognition and religious respect, which most of the Afghan Taliban acquired while waging jihad against perceived "infidels" such as the Soviets Union and the US. This study suggests that the current Salafism phenomenon in the Pashtun area is not temporary, but permanent, bringing with it changes to both the tribal and leadership structure. Some Sunni Islamic beliefs have the potential to endure, permanently transforming the local religious, political, social, and cultural structure of the tribes. The preeminent position of these Amirs appears to be permanent in the Pashtun society and not transitional as was predicted in the past. It is argued in this study that some new Salafist Sunni Islam can bring positive changes to Pashtun society if it remains peaceful. However, it may get deadly and violent if the Salafists try to impose their will on the local society as they did in the extremely violent insurgency they conducted in Swat or in some parts of FATA and southern Afghanistan.

This study is about Pashtun tribes and their attraction to Salafism. There are numerous brands of Salafism which the author has observed and which will be discussed in detail in a later section. In this study, Salafism or Salafi Islam describes a form of Sunni Islam that Tablighi Jamaat preaches and practices in the Pashtun inhabited areas. It describes the religious aspects of tribal village life to address the following questions. What were the religious practices prevalent among the Pashtun tribes in this village? Were they tolerant and secular in nature? How have some of these practices changed and why? What were the drivers of this religious change from the Hanafi Sufi School to a more rigid Salafi practice? Who took the lead in this change? Who was the catalyst for this change? Is an introduction of this new religious ideology causing tension between the local tribesmen? What is driving this new change in the community? Are Pashtun tribes descending toward more rigid Salafism and why? What is the future of these tribes as they gravitate toward Salafism? Are they going to be prone to the religious current championed by Al-Qa'ida and their allies who are using violent means to attempt to bring about political change in the Muslim world and beyond? What will it mean for the stability and security of the Pashtun inhabited areas in Pakistan and Afghanistan? What will it mean for the stability of the governments of Pakistan and Afghanistan?

Methodology

In this study the participant observation method was used because this method provides a detailed understanding of the Pashtun society, and the anthropological data concerning the local tribes, religious practices by the tribesmen, and local religious and tribal leaders, required close observation as a participant in order for the context of outcomes to be fully understood. The participant observation method was

9

supplemented with a survey of the entire village, which collected basic demographic and economic information. Since there were only approximately 700 households in the village of Pak Kaya, the survey covered the whole village.

The village of Qoz Kaya in the Swabi district was selected for this study because this village is a classic Pashtun village inhabited by only one dominant tribe, the Jehangir Khel, village with very strong tribal structure. The tribesmen were also very strong supporters of Sufism. All of the village inhabitants used to practice Sufism before the Tablighi Jamaat made inroads into the village. The author has witnessed this first hand during his stay in Qoz Kaya from April 1991-1993, and during numerous visits to the village between 1993 and 2012. This mixture of strong tribal, social, political, religious and cultural structure in the village provided an excellent laboratory for this case study. Some historical data used in the study was collected through village informants.

A descriptive method was used in the research because the study required detailed analysis of the tribesmen, their religious practices, and the roles of both young and old tribesmen. In addition, descriptive and qualitative methods help present in more detail the people's participation in the decision-making process and the leadership. Since this study requires case examples to answer questions raised, the qualitative method was believed to provide a more accurate description of these cases.

This study is based on a series of case studies the author observed since the 1980s. The author lived in the village off and on since that time, annually visiting for three to four weeks at a time since his departure. The observation and participation methods were supplemented by informal interviews with the local residents to verify the facts and obtain additional details of the past events.

A Process of Social and Religious Change in the Pashtun Society

Over the last few decades, the communities along the Pakistan and Afghanistan borderland have been going through social, political, economic, and cultural changes. The drivers of these changes appear to be modern education, access to cities, a modern communication system, and employment opportunities in the service economy. The drivers of change appear to be transforming the local religious ideology from a more moderate Sufism to a more restrictive Salafism. This conversion from Sufism to Salafism appears to be drastically changing local Pashtun tribal and social structure. This study argues that this conversion from Sufism to Salafism appears to be peaceful in certain Pashtun areas but violent in others. It is also demonstrated in this study that unless and until this conversion is managed by the local governments, the process may get violent. This has already begun to happen in some parts of Pashtun inhabited areas in Pakistan and Afghanistan, especially along the border shared with Pakistan where consistent levels of conflict have occurred for over a decade.

This study also notes that a conversion from a more tolerant Sufism to a more restrictive Salafism would continue to transform local Pashtun tribal structure. It is argued that unlike past transformations, which were temporary, as with Ahmad Shah Shaheed, Hadda Mullah, and the Powindah Mullah, this current change appears to be permanent. This conversion from

11

Sufism to Salafism has the capacity to reconfigure Pashtun tribal structure, fueling internal strife and fissures in the society. This internal strife and fissures are likely to destabilize the region, inviting into the local political and religious mix more radical and violent Salafists including Al-Qa'ida.

This study notes that institutions which in the past, stimulated modernity and tolerance in society appear to be causing this major transformation from Sufism to Salafism. Interestingly, the forces of modernization—city life, education a service economy, and communication—appear to be the major forces behind this religious change. The religious change in turn appears to be eroding the Pashtun traditional structure, a major source of stability and peace in the area.

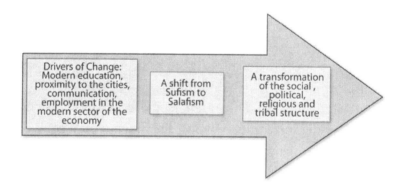

Figure 2. Process of Social and Religious Transformation.

It is explained in this book that instead of secularizing or liberalizing the local population, the forces of modernity and modern institutions—city life, modern education, modern communication and a service economy—are pushing the locals toward Salafism throughout the Pakistan and Afghanistan borderland. It is possible that in times of rapid transformation,

12

the local people turn to religion for answers. This transformation from the old religious order to a new one has undermined a delicate religious, social, tribal, and political balance within Pashtun society, and has also created wedges at the family, tribal, and societal levels. In addition, this transformation has undermined the delicate equilibrium among the three main components of traditional Pashtun society—the Mullahs, the Pirs, and the traditional Tribal leaders.

There are tribesmen within each community who continue to practice their old religious rituals and continue to adhere to traditional tribal values, while others, mainly the newest generation of educated, technologically savvy, cosmopolitan young men, have been abandoning the old religious practices, and adopting Salafism. Salafism is defined here as an ideology which is practiced by both peaceful religious groups like the Tablighi Jamaat in the South Asia and by more radical groups like Al-Qa'ida, Tehrik-i Taliban Pakistan, the Afghan Taliban and other militant groups like Lashker-e-Taiba (*see* Appendix B). The Deobandi ideology preached by the Darul Uloom Deoband Madrassa in northern India and the Sunni Islamic Wahhabi practices followed in the Saudi Arabia provide the ideological foundation to Sunni Salafism. The concept of Salafism will be explained in details in a later section of this book. While different Salafist groups may differ in their interpretations of Islam's foundational documents, all of them agree on the basic principles that rejects Sufism and Sufi practices. The Salafists also undermine the traditional religious and tribal leaders, creating instability.

Is it possible that both forces—the old Sufism and traditional tribalism and the new Salafism—could co-exist peacefully? Or will this division turn into a violent confrontation, which has already occurred in the FATA, most of Afghanistan's provinces, and in Swat?

Answers to these questions depend upon the will and capacity of the local governments. There are two key drivers that may be required to prevent violent confrontation between these competing forces. First, there is a need for a powerful security force, which is capable and willing to ensure the peaceful coexistence without siding with either one of these groups. Second, this security force needs to allow these two forces to preach their ideology and practices peacefully and freely, but they must manage, rather than suppress, the evolutionary process by letting these groups operate peacefully.

In the absence of these two conditions, the local Pashtun societies are likely to descend into chaos, triggering a violent confrontation and destabilizing local areas. It is possible that new Salafists led by young men could impose their will on the Sufis, triggering a confrontation between the two groups. For example, in Khyber Agency, the Salafist group Lashkar-e-Islam tried to force the Sufis to comply with the tenets of Salafism, triggering an open war between the two groups. Both the Sufi tribes and the Salafi tribes have organized themselves into Lashkar-e-Islam (LI), a Salafist group, and Ansar-ul-Islam (AI), a Sufi group. Both LI and AL have been fighting with each other since 2005. A small number of Afridi tribemen have also aligned themselves with Amar bil Maroof Wa Nahi Ul Munkar also known as Hajji Namdar group, a radical Salafist outfit with strong ties to the Al-Qa'ida. This group operates only in Qambar Khel sub-tribe of the Afridi tribe in Khyber.

At the village level, Salafists and Sufis may resort to violence against one another, drawing their extended families and the local tribes into the fight. In Pashtun society, a tribe is expected to back a tribal member, and an extended family is expected to stand by its members. This tribal and social obligation may force every tribesman to align himself with either the Salafist group or the Sufi group.

For example, in Khyber Agency, some families from the Qambar Khel, a sub-tribe of the Afridi tribe, supported the Salafists. Some families from the Malik Din Khel, another sub-tribe of the Afridi tribe, supported the Sufis. Beginning in the late 1990s the entire Qambar Khel tribe became Salafist. The Qambar Khel Salafists were divided into Lashkar-e-Islam and the Amar bil Maroof Wa Nahi Ul Munkar group. **Predictably,** the local Pakistani press in March 2011 reported that these Salafists groups were fighting with each other.

Lashkar–e-Islam has also been fighting with Ansar-ul-Islam and this struggle has spread across the Afridi tribe. The Zakka Khel, Kuki Khel, Malik Din Khel, Qambar Khel, Sepah and Adam Aka Khel sub-tribes of the Afridis were drawn into the fight between Lashkar-e-Islam and Ansar-ul-Islam. As of April 2011, some of the Zakka Khel and Adam Aka Khel sub-tribes had deserted Lashkar-e-Islam after one of the prominent Zakka Khel tribesmen was killed by Lashkar-e-Islam members, according to the local Pakistani press. The Daily Times reported on April 11, 2012 that Lashkar-e-Islam militants shot dead five Zakka Khel in Bara on April 11. They also slaughtered two of their former cadres. Among those killed were a former 'commander' Hazrat Khan, and his friend, Rehman. Sources told the Daily Times that the victims had recently started supporting

Security Forces in an effort to bring peace to the area. Two people lost their lives and another two were also injured in a gun battle between Lashkar-e-Islam and Tawheed-ul-Islam, another unknown Salafist group, in Tirah Valley.[22]

The Tribe and its Religious Environment

The village of Pak Kaya is located in the heart of Swabi district, one of the key districts of Khyber Pakhtunkhwa. There are a number of prominent madrassas in Swabi district. Two madrassas—Shahmansoor madrassa and Panj Pir Madrassa—are the most famous religious seminaries in Swabi and are located between four and five miles from the village. Both madrassas have been traditional rivals despite the fact that both are Deobandi Salafi madrassas. The Panj Pir madrassa preaches a more intolerant, restricted, radical Salafi ideology while the Shahmansoor madrassa teaches a more tolerant form of Islam.

Most of the locals followed the tenets of the Shahmansoor madrassa, because they view the Panj Pir madrassa as a Wahhabi madrassa. The head of the madrassa, Sheikh ul Quran Allama Muhammad Tayyib Tahir Panjpiri (also known as Tahir Saib) is a Wahhabi, a derogative label among the local Pashtuns. The Wahhabi label is used to portray someone as an extreme Salafist. Most of the Muslims in Saudi Arabia follow a restrictive version of Islam known as Wahhabi Islam. The word is associated with Abdul Wahab, who

---

[22] Full details are available in "The Daily Times" (Islamabad), April 6, 2012.

16

supported the Saudi royal family to gain power in Saudi Arabia in 1930s, and his teaching.

Shahmansoor Madrassa:

Shahmansoor Madrassa is located in Shahmansoor village, between four and five miles from Pak Kaya. The villagers reported that Mullah Koka Ustad started the madrassa, and his son Noorul Hadi is the current head of the madrassa.

The Jehangir Khel tribesmen and the village's Mullah Mustafa look to Shahmansoor Madrassa for religious guidance. For example, the Jehangir Khel and Mustafa observed the start and the end of the Muslim holy month of Ramadan based on the order from the Shahmansoor Madrassa. The Jehangir Khel tribe does not follow the restrictive Salafism practiced and taught at the Panj Pir Madrassa and does not follow the guidance of the Madrassa when it comes to religious matters, including the start and the end of Ramadan.

Shahmansoor Madrassa is a large facility located at the edge of Shahmansoor village in Swabi district, about 90 kilometers from the Pakistani capital of Islamabad. It is located on the right side of the Jehangira – Swabi highway.

Panj Pir Madrassa:

Panj Pir Madrassa is located in Panj Pir village. Tahir Saib is the head of the madrassa. The Jehangir Khel tribesmen view the Panj Pir Madrassa and its Mullah as Wahhabi. Even Pak Kaya village's Mullah Mustafa does not look to Tahir Saib for any religious guidance. Rather, Mullah Mustafa follows the Shahmansoor Madrassa and Koka Ustad's son.

Most of the students in Panj Pir Madrassa are reported to be Afghans especially from Kunar, Nangarhar, and Nuristan Provinces. Other students come from Swat, Dir, Mohmand and Bajaur Agencies of Pakistan. Some people called the region the Panj Pir Arc.

In contrast, most of the students in Shahmansoor Madrassa are Pakistanis from the immediate region. There are some Afghan students. Panj Pir Madrassa has been noted to be a champion of jihad in Afghanistan and its graduated included Sufi Mohammad, Faqir Mohammad, and numerous other extremists. In contrast, Shahmansoor Madrassa does not preach violent jihad.

Panj Pir Madrassa appears to have more resources and it is also larger in size than the Shahmansoor Madrassa. Local villagers believe that Panj Pir Madrassa receives financial support from the Saudi Arabia and other Gulf donors. Panj Pir Madrassa also receives money from the government of Pakistan, according to the locals, who also believe that Pakistani security agencies have provided financial support to Panj Pir Madrassa in the past. Major Amir, an ex-ISI officer, is a nephew of Tahir Saib. A review of sermons by Mullah Tahir Saib on YouTube revealed a significant emphasis on jihad by the cleric. For example, Sheikhulquran Muhammad Tayyib Tahiri Panjpir in an Ijtema 2011 openly supported the Taliban and their jihad in Afghanistan.[23] Pakistani press revealed that a significant numbers of militant commanders in the region graduated from Panj Pir Madrassa. For example, Mangal Bagh, the head of Lashkar-i-

---

[23] http://www.youtube.com/watch?v=qa9Ljwp9GcE

Islam in Khyber Agency, was a student at the Panj Pir Madrassa. Mullah Fazlullah, the head of Tehrik-e-Taliban Pakistan in Swat, was also a graduate of Panj Pir Madrassa. A significant numbers of Afghan Taliban commanders also graduated from the Panj Pir Madrassa, according to the locals.

It is worth noting here that presence of two important Madaris[24] has nothing to do with the inroad by the Tablighi Jamaat into Pak Kaya village. None of the local Amirs studied at the madaris. The leading Amirs in the village attended modern educational institutions and none of them have any madrassa schooling. While these madrassas may have an impact on the militancy and insurgency in Afghanistan and other parts of Pakistan, they have no impact on Pak Kaya. These religious schools are explained here because these two institutions have been sowing the seeds of Salafism in the area for decades. The Tablighi Jamaat amirs have been acting as vanguards of this Salafist inroad, which was initiated in these two madrassas and accelerated the spread of extremism in the region.

The new generations of mullahs in the surrounding villages are graduates of these madaris. In Friday prayers, these mullahs openly preach a restrictive version of Salafism, combined with violent jihad. There is a clearly visible change in the local tribesmen's lives. For example, almost all the tribesmen would shave their beard before marriage. Now, one can't see a young man without beard. In the past, the young men would arrange bachelor parties during marriage and invite female dancers. Now, no one can arrange a bachelor party. Salafists

---

[24] Maderi is the plural of madrassa.

banned all the social entertainment practiced by the tribes, including bachelor parties, music, dog fights, and similar forms of entertainment.

The Role of the Mullah's Family in the Tribe

There are two prominent mullah families in Pak Kaya village—Mullah Mustafa's family and Mullah Mohammad Omar's family. Mustafa's family is viewed as the Jehangir Khel's mullah family and out of respect, the locals call him Laljee (older, respected brother). The villagers support the family financially by providing five percent of their agriculture proceeds to Mustafa's family. This percentage is known as "usher," an Islamic religious tax on the agriculture products. In addition, each family is required to pay "Fitrana," an Islamic religious donation, during the "Eid Bakra" or "Big Eid." It is an Islamic religious requirement that each family that can afford it must pay 10 Rupees (about 8 cents) for each family member. For example, a family with 10 members is required to pay 100 Rupees to the Mullah. Mustafa's family depends on these two sources of income.

In return, Mustafa extends numerous services to the tribesmen. He maintains mosque, leads prayers five times a day, washes the bodies of the dead, leads funerals, and teaches the Koran to the young boys. Mustafa's wife teaches the Koran to the girls. Mustafa delivers a Friday sermon at the village mosque, but he does not raise the issue of Deobandism vs. Sufism publicly in his sermon. Mustafa was observed to not raise political or controversial topics in his Friday sermons, but privately he would express his views against the Pirs and their practices, which he viewed as un-Islamic.

The tribesmen who continued to believe in Sufism chant "Zakir" (loudly recited praise to Prophet Muhammad) but Mullah Mustafa was against this practice, because he believed the "Zakir" was forbidden in Islam but he would not challenge the tribesmen to stop for fear of losing his position in the village. Mullah Omar and his brother Shah Mohammad were very vocal against the "Zakir" and other practices of the Pirs, however they were not powerful enough to stop the Sufi practices. Despite the fact that the mullah's family was living among the Jehangir Khel as a dependent family, they were totally shunned by the tribe. Both brothers were banned from leading the prayers in the Jehangir Khel mosque and became imams in a nearby village. Since Jehangir Khel shunned Mullah Omar, he became a prayer leader in Bar Kaya. Mustafa did not attempt to stop the tribesmen from practicing the Sufi practices because he was afraid of losing his job as a mullah of the village.

In 2009, Mustafa requested that the Jehangir Khel accept his son, as his successor since Mustafa's son had received his advanced religious education from a Deobandi madrassa in Punjab. Mustafa's son was not only a Deobandi mufti, the highest position within the Sunni Islamic clerical hierarchy, but he was also an active member of the Tablighi Jamaat. Mustafa knew that his son has to be approved by the jirga of Jehangir tribe, an assembly of elders from about dozen of families. Two of those—Hajji and Khabli—were the most powerful families. Mustafa needed the support of both Hajji and Khabli families for a favorable decision from the Jehangir Khel jirga.

The Hajji family, one of the most power families in Jehangir Khel tribe, accepted the proposed appointment of

Mustafa's son as a future Imam of the mosque, while the Khabli family, which was also one of the power families and a rival to the Hajji family, opposed Mustafa's son appointment. The rest of the Jehangir Khel families agreed to the appointment of Mustafa's son as their future Imam.

Like other decisions in the village, one family could veto a decision affecting the whole Jehangir Khel since all the families within the Jehangir Khel must agree to Mustafa's son's appointment as the future Imam of the mosque. The Khabli family opposed Mustafa's son because he was perceived to be too close to the Hajji's family. It was a part of power struggle between the two powerful families—the Hajji family and the Khabli family. The tribesmen revealed that the Khabli family opposed Mustafa's son as an Imam because he was a Salafist. With the exception of Amir Hanif Khan and his brothers from the Khabli, who were active members of the Tablighi Jamaat, the whole family was committed to Sufism. They thought that any appointment of Mustafa's son would further reduce the influence of Sufism and could tilt the balance in favor of the Salafists.

After long protracted lobbying and arm-twisting, the Khabli family agreed to the appointment of Mustafa's son. Mustafa was seen grooming his son to the important position of Imam and Mustafa's son avoided controversial issues during the Friday sermons. Mustafa's son was also observed to be leading some of prayers. The appointment of Mustafa's son clearly gave the Tablighi Jamaat an advantage over the Sufi group in the village and the Amirs of Tablighi Jamaat were happy about this appointment because the Imam would give them access to the mosque, a focal point between the Salafists and the Sufis.

A Brief Definition of Sufism and Salafism

In this section, a brief introduction of Sufism and Salafism (the Tablighi Jamaat) is presented for the readers. The principal tenet of Salafism is that the Islam that was preached by Muhammad and practiced by his Companions, as well as the second and third generations succeeding them, was pure, unadulterated, and, therefore, the ultimate authority for the interpretation of the two sources of revelation given to Muhammad, namely the Qur'an and the Sunnah. As noted earlier, this book is not about Sufism and Salafist Tablighi Jamaat. This book is about the Pashtun tribes and what drives these tribes to gravitate toward the Tabligh Jamaat and the Salafism. [25]

A practitioner of Sufism is generally known as a Sufi or a Dervish. Classical Sufis would recite Zakir, a practice of repeating the names of God, and asceticism. Most scholars note that the Sufi Orders, which are either Sunni or Shia or mixed in doctrine, trace many of their original precepts from the Muhammad through his cousin Ali, with the notable exception of the Naqshbandi who trace their origins through the first Caliph, Abu Bakr.

Sufism: Sufi orders include the Qadiria Boutshishia, Oveyssi, Naqshbandi, the Chishti, the Qadiriyyah, the Qalandariyya, the Sarwari Qadiri, the Shadhliyya and the

---

[25] Moosa, Ebrahim *"Ghazali And The Poetics Of Imagination"*, by ISBN 0-8078-5612-6, p. 21.

Suhrawardiyya. Following are some of the practices of Sufis.[26] Some Sufi orders engage in ritualized zakir ceremonies: recitation, singing including Qawwali, music of the Indian subcontinent, instrumental music, dance, (most famously the Sufi whirling of the Mevlevi order), incense, meditation, ecstasy, and trances.

Muraqaba, which means the vigilant, is a practice of meditation. Through muraqaba, a person watches over or takes care of the spiritual heart, acquires knowledge about it, and becomes attuned to the Divine Presence, which is ever vigilant. In popular Sufism practice is to visit the tombs of saints, great scholars, and righteous people. This is a particularly common practice in South Asia, where famous tombs include those of Khoja Afāq, near Kashgar, in China; Lal Shahbaz Qalander, in Sindh, Pakistan; Moinuddin Chishti in Ajmer, India. Music and dance is a part of Sufi tradition. Famous Sufi singers from the Indian subcontinent include Nusrat Fateh Ali Khan, Kailash Kher, Alam Lohar, Abida Parveen. A. R. Rahman. Bangara and Kawali. [27 28 29 30 31]

[26] Moosa, Ebrahim "Ghazali And The Poetics Of Imagination", ISBN 0-8078-5612-6, Page 21.
[27] Ibid, page 21.
[28] Dr Baker, Abdul-Haqq, "Extremists in Our Midst: Confronting Terror", Palgrave Macmillan, 2011
[29] Meijer, Roel, "Global Salafism: Islam's New Religious Movement. Columbia University Press, 2009 pp. 34. ISBN 978-0-231-15420-8
[30] "Jihad" By Gilles Kepel, Anthony F. Roberts. Books.google.com. 2006-02-24. ISBN 978-1-84511-257-8. http://books.google.com/?id=OLvTNk75hUoC&dq=islamism&printsec=frontcover. Retrieved 2010-04-18
[31] "Dawat-us-Salafiyyah (Call of those who preceded us)". Muttaqun.com

Salafism: The principal tenet of Salafism is that "the Islam that was preached by Muhammad and practiced by his Companions, as well as the second and third generations succeeding them, was pure, unadulterated, and, therefore, the ultimate authority for the interpretation of the two sources of revelation given to Muhammad, namely the Qur'an and the Sunnah." In this book, Salafism refers to the practices of the Tablighi Jamaat, a proselytizing movement in the South Asia. Tablighi Jamaat is a transnational religious movement.

Muhammad Ilyas started this movement in 1926 in Mewat, north India, an area inhabited by Rajput tribes known as Meos. At the time, some Muslim Indian leaders feared that Muslims were losing their religious identity to the majority Hindu culture. The movement primarily aims at Islamic spiritual reformation by working at the grass roots level, reaching out to Muslims across all social and economic spectrums to bring them closer to the practices of Islamic prophet Muhammad.

Tablighi Jamaat

Tablighi Jamaat came forth as an offshoot of the Deobandi movement. Dar Ul Uloom Deoband is a religious seminary in India which preaches Salafism. Tablighi Jamaat maintains a non-affiliating stature in matters of politics and fiqh (jurisprudence) so as to eschew the controversies that would otherwise accompany such affiliations. Tablighi Jamaat has largely avoided electronic media and has emphasized a personal communication for proselytizing. Tablighi Jamaat's role as a springboard to terrorist organizations has been questioned several times but there is no evidence that the Tablighi Jamaat deliberately act as a recruiting arm for Islamic militant organizations. [32] [33] [34] [35] [36]

Tablighi Jamaat defines its objective with reference to the concept of Da'wa which literally means 'to call' and connotes to an invitation to act. Tablighi ethic discourages social enmeshments in customary and ceremonial rituals, which are usually extravagantly followed in South Asia.

Six Principles of Tablighi Jamaat:

Tablighi Jamaat organizes jamaat (Assembly) of at least ten persons and sends them to various villages. Once in a village, this Jamaat would invite the local Muslims to assemble in the mosque and present their message in the form of Six Principles.

Kalimah: An article of faith in which the Tabligh accepts that "there is no god but Allah and the Muhammad (Sallalaho Alihe Wasalam) is His messenger.

---

[32] Moosa, Ebrahim, *"Ghazali And The Poetics Of Imagination"*, ISBN 0-8078-5612-6, Page 21

[33] Baker, Dr Abdul-Haqq, *'Extremists in Our Midst: Confronting Terror,"* Palgrave Macmillan, 2011

[34] Meijer, Roel (2009). "Introduction". In Meijer, Roel. *Global Salafism: Islam's New Religious Movement*. Columbia University Press. pp. 34. ISBN 978-0-231-15420-8

[35] "Jihad" By Gilles Kepel, Anthony F. Roberts. Books.google.com. 2006-02-24. ISBN 978-1-84511-257-8. http://books.google.com/?id=OLvTNk75hUoC&dq=islamism&printsec= frontcover. Retrieved 2010-04-18

[36] "Dawat-us-Salafiyyah (Call of those who preceded us)". Muttaqun.com

Salah: Five daily prayers, which are essential to spiritual elevation, piety, and a life free from the ills of the material world.

Ilm and Zakir: "The knowledge and remembrance of Allah conducted in sessions in which the congregation listens to preaching by the emir, performs prayers, recites the Quran and reads the Hadith. Ikram-i-Muslim means "the treatment of Muslims with honor and deference."

Tas'hih-i-Niyyat: is "reforming one's life in supplication to Allah by performing every human action for the sake of Allah and toward the goal of self-transformation."

Tafrigh-i-Waqt: is defined as "the sparing of time to live a life based on faith and learning its virtues, following in the footsteps of the Prophet, and taking His message door-to-door for the sake of faith." [37] [38] [39] [40] [41]

Tablighi Jamaat follows an informal organizational structure and keeps an introverted institutional profile. As an

---

[37] Moosa, Ebrahim, *"Ghazali And The Poetics Of Imagination"*, ISBN 0-8078-5612-6, Page 21

[38] Baker, Dr Abdul-Haqq, *"Extremists in Our Midst: Confronting Terror,"* Palgrave Macmillan, 2011

[39] Meijer, Roel (2009). "Introduction". In Meijer, Roel. *Global Salafism: Islam's New Religious Movement.* Columbia University Presss. pp. 34. ISBN 978-0-231-15420-8

[40] "Jihad" By Gilles Kepel, Anthony F. Roberts. Books.google.com. 2006-02-24. ISBN 978-1-84511-2578. http://books.google.com/?id=OLvTNk75hUoC&dq=islamism&printsec=frontcover. Retrieved 2010-04-18

[41] "Dawat-us-Salafiyyah (Call of those who preceded us)". Muttaqun.com

organization Tablighi Jamaat does not seek donations and is largely funded by its senior members. A collection of books, usually referred as the Tablighi Nisaab (Tablighi Curriculum), are recommended by Tablighi Jamaat's elders for general reading. This set includes three books: (Hayatus Sahaba, Fazail-e-Amal, Fazail-e-Sadqaat and Muntakhab-e-Ahadis).

The organization's activities are coordinated through centers and headquarters called Markaz. Tablighi Jamaat maintains its international headquarters, called Nizamuddin Markaz, in the Nizamuddin West district of New Delhi, India, where it originally started. It also has centers in over 120 countries which coordinate its activities. These headquarters organize jamaats and preaching missions which are self-funded by their respective members

Leadership

Amir is the title of leadership in the Tablighi. The Amir of Tablighi Jamaat is appointed for life by the central consultative council (Shura) and elders of Tablighi Jamaat. The first Amir, also the founder, was Muhammad Ilyas. The second was his son Muhammad Yusuf and the third was Inaam ul Hasan. At present, there is a council of three people Zubair ul Hasan, Saad Kandhalawi and Haji Muhammad Abdul Wahhaab sahib, who collectively serve as Amir.

These individual jamaats, each led by an Amir, are sent from each markaz across the city or country. The duration of the work depends upon the discretion of each jamaat. A trip can take an evening, a couple of days or a much longer. Tablighi Jamaat encourages its followers to spend "one night a week, one weekend a month, 40 continuous days a year, and ultimately 120 days at least once in their lives engaged in Tablighi missions". During the course of these missions, members are generally seen dressed in simple, white, loose clothing, carrying sleeping bags on their backs. These members use mosques as their base during this travel but particular mosques, due to more frequent Tablighi activities, have come to be specifically associated with Tablighi Jamaat. During their stay in mosques, these jamaats conduct a daily gasht, which involves visiting local neighborhoods, preferably with the help of a guide. They invite people to attend the Maghrib prayer at the mosque where they hear a sermon after the prayers which essentially outlines the Six Principles noted above. The members of the Jamaat are assigned different roles based on the day's *mashwara* or consultation. The markaz keeps records of each *jamaat* and its members.

An annual gathering of followers, called *ijtema*, is summoned to the headquarters of the respective countries. A typical *ijtema* continues for three days and ends with an exceptionally long prayer. The largest of such annual gatherings are held in India, Pakistan and Bangladesh. The Bengali gathering, called *Bishwa Ijtema* (World Gathering) includes followers from around the world. It is held in Tongi near Dhaka, Bangladesh with an attendance exceeding 2 million people. The second largest Tablighi Jamaat gathering takes place in Raiwind, Pakistan attended by approximately 2 million people. [42, 43]

---

[42] Moosa, Ebrahim, *"Ghazali And The Poetics Of Imagination"*, ISBN 0-8078-5612-6, p. 21.

[43] Baker, Dr Abdul-Haqq, " *Extremists in Our Midst: Confronting Terror,"* Palgrave Macmillan, 2011

The first *jamaat* of women was formed in Nizamuddin, Delhi. As long as they are accompanied by a close male relative women are encouraged to go out in jamaats and work among other women and family members while following the rules of modesty and seclusion.

The Pashtun Tribes and Different Types of Salafism

As noted earlier, there are different strands of Salafism practiced in the Pashtun inhabited areas of Pakistan and Afghanistan. Despite this, the underlying ideology of Salafism is the same. The tactics of preaching and enforcing Salafism may vary from one group to another or from one region to another. In the village of Pak Kaya, the Tablighi Jamaat is the face of Salafism. The Tablighi Jamaat and its members have been very peaceful in the village, for now, and they have condemned the violent actions of the Taliban and Al-Qa'ida.

The Taliban claim to be Deobandi/Salafi Muslims and the Taliban and Al-Qa'ida's ideology is consistent with the Tablighi Jamaat. However, the Tablighi Jamaat is against the practices of the Taliban and Al-Qa'ida. The Taliban emerged in the early 1990s from Pakistani religious seminaries, and by 1996, conquered most of Afghanistan. The Taliban installed an oppressive totalitarian regime in Afghanistan. Between 2002 and 2008, the Taliban's ally, Muttahida Majlis-e-Amal (MMA), the United Action Front, that consisted of Jamaat Islami (JI), Jamiat Ulema-e-Pakistan (N), a Barelvi school of Sunni Muslims, Jamiat Ulema-e-Islam , Jamiat Ulema-e-Islam (F) , Jamiat Ulema-e-Islam (S)], which represents the Deobandi school, Jamiat-e-Ahle Hadith and Tehrik-e-Jafria Pakistan, a Shia party known now as Pakistan Islami Tehrik, controlled the Pakistani border provinces of Khyber Pakhtunkhwa and Baluchistan. MMA provided the necessary safe havens to the Taliban and Al Qai'da members, who retreated from Afghanistan in aftermath of the United States' attack on Afghanistan.

After the September 11, 2001 attack by Al-Qa'ida, the US and a coalition of anti-Taliban Tajiks called the Northern Alliance, toppled the Taliban and installed Hamid Karzai, a pro-US Pashtun leader from the Popalzai tribe as the president of Afghanistan. After the defeat, some Taliban laid down their weapons and melted into the Afghan population, while others went to Pakistan, where they had lived as refugees during the Soviet occupation of Afghanistan in 1980s. By 2004, the Taliban reconstituted themselves as a formidable insurgent movement in the region, waging a violent campaign against the US and NATO forces in Afghanistan from their safe havens in the Pashtun areas. The Taliban movement in Afghanistan has also spread to the western border area of Pakistan, commonly known as the FATA and Khyber Pakhtunkhwa, threatening the state of Pakistan, a nuclear power with a current population of 170 million people. In May 2009, the Pakistani military began a major military operation in Swat valley, once known as a paradise due to its beautiful mountains, forcing millions of people to flee Swat and Buner districts. In October 2009, the Pakistani military launched another major military operation against the Taliban, this time in South Waziristan, the military headquarters for the Pakistani Taliban, who have been fighting under an umbrella organization known as Tehrik-e-Taliban Pakistan (TTP). The Taliban retaliated with a violent bombing campaign in Pakistan, killing hundreds of people in major cities, to include Islamabad, Rawalpindi, Peshawar, and Lahore.

The Taliban's ideology consists of a set of rules and rituals based on the local Pashtun culture known as Pakhtunwali combined with the Deobandi/Salafi brand of Sunni Islam. Talibanization is a term coined following the rise of the Taliban's religious movement in Afghanistan referring to the process where other religious movements come to follow the restrictive practices of the Taliban. In its original usage, Talibanization referred to an ideology followed by Islamic militant groups along the Pakistan-Afghanistan borderland who followed Afghan Taliban practices. These includes forbidding employment and schooling for women, banning activities generally tolerated by other Muslims, such as movies, television, videos, music, dancing, hanging pictures in homes, clapping during sports events, requiring men to have beards, enforcement of its regulations using armed "religious police", destruction of non-Muslim artifacts, especially carvings and statues and Sufi Shrines, and a discriminatory attitude towards non-Muslims and Shia Muslims.

The Taliban, for example, forbade the tribesmen from listening to music, indulging in any kind of romantic relationship outside marriage, and forbade the tribesmen from following Sufism. The Taliban punished those who broke these rules, including beheadings in public stadiums, corporal punishment in public places, and cutting of the hands and the ears of those who committed lesser violations of their laws.

Talibanization has been spreading to other parts of Pakistan, raising fears among the Western capitals that the Taliban may ultimately gain control of the country. The local Taliban have spread their influence as far as Peshawar and Southern Punjab. The local Taliban's influence on the Pakistani border provinces has given the Taliban in Afghanistan, as well as Al-Qa'ida, a strategic depth in the region, threatening the US and NATO forces in Afghanistan and undermining the writ of both the Pakistani and Afghan governments.

The Taliban has enforced their strict Islamic views in the areas they control. The Pakistani government, under pressure from the Taliban, in April 2009 promulgated the Sharia laws in the Swat valley, a border district in the KP, to appease the local Taliban. The Pakistani government's concession emboldened the Taliban, who took control of neighboring Buner district an area located about 60 miles away from the capital Islamabad. In summer 2009, realizing the inherent danger of this Taliban presence so close to Islamabad, and under pressure from the US and Europe, the Pakistani military launched a major military operation against the Taliban in Swat and Buner. By the end of summer 2009, the military had cleared most of Swat and Buner of Taliban, which resulted in the return of almost all Internally Displaced People (IDPs) from refugee camps to their original villages.

The mainstream Sunni Islamic religious clerics considered Talibanization as "Kharjis," (heresy) because the Taliban narrowly interpret Sharia laws. In addition, the Taliban's enforcement mechanisms are not in legal agreement with Sharia laws. In Swat, for example, in early April 2009, the Taliban lashed a young girl, who allegedly had an affair with a local boy, according to local and international press.[44] The Taliban spokesman from Swat defended the Taliban's action and was

---

[44] http://www.guardian.co.uk/world/2009/apr/02/taliban-pakistan-justice-women-flogging

quoted as saying that the militants showed mercy to both the girl and the boy after they agreed to marry each other. The spokesman added that according to his interpretation of the Sharia laws, they were punishable by stoning because both committed adultery.

Similar stories about the high-handedness of the Taliban were very common in the Pashtun areas of Pakistan and Afghanistan. The Taliban enforced one of the most rigid and narrow interpretations of Islam on the tribesmen. The Taliban also reconstituted a powerful insurgent movement in the area, in addition to waging a violent insurgency in Pakistan and Afghanistan.

Some local tribesmen support the Taliban because the militants give them money, badly needed weapons and explosive expertise, and extra muscle. The tribesmen use these resources to enhance their power against their enemies. The foreigners also give money and weapons to the Afghan Taliban, as well as providing jihadists to join their cause. The Afghan Taliban gives these foreigners an opportunity to fight the coalition forces and become martyrs.

There are four different kinds of Salafists in the region. One group of Salafists is non-Pashtun and is affiliated with Al-Qa'ida. The Second group of Salafists is associated with the Afghan insurgency and they are called the Taliban. The third group of Salafists operates under an umbrella organization known as TTP. In addition to these three militant Salafists, there is a fourth group called the Tablighi Jamaat that currently seems to concentrate only on peaceful proselytizing.

The non-Pashtun jihadi Salafists mainly come from cities, educated in the modern colleges and universities, and are from middle and upper classes. In contrast, the Afghan Taliban is comprised of mainly poor Pashtun families from rural areas and refugee camps and its members attended religious madrassas in Pakistan. The local Taliban affiliated with TTP come mainly from rural villages. They received their education either in madrassas or in modern institutions and they claim to be Tablighi Amirs, an assertion denied by the senior leadership of Tablighi Jamaat. The senior members of the Tablighi Jamaat are highly educated and cosmopolitan in their lifestyle. Most of them come from relatively richer middle and upper classes. Almost all the Tablighi Amirs in the area of Pak Kaya were observed to be from prominent feudal families. These Amirs enjoy religious, social, tribal and political influence within society. They were observed to be credible voices.

Each and every Salafist group operating in Pakistan-Afghanistan borderland has a different agenda. The non-Pashtun extremists mainly affiliated with Al-Qa'ida are in the region to fight the coalition forces and the US. Most of these foreigners are the part of the al-Qaida network. Al-Qa'ida has a global agenda—attacking near enemies, the US allies in the region, and the far enemy, the US. These Al-Qa'ida affiliated militants don't get involved in local tribal matters however in some cases, they do mediate conflict between or among the local militants, which further enhances Al-Qa'ida's prestige and influence.

In contrast, the Afghan Taliban is fighting an insurgency against coalition forces. Unlike Al-Qa'ida, the Afghan Taliban does not have a global agenda. The TTP's goal is to establish a society free of social crimes and an Islamic regime in Pakistan and Afghanistan. TTP believes that the Pashtun society is poisoned by the widespread influence of western culture through media, DVDs and movies, modern education, and consumerism. They struggle to create a pure Pashtun society reminiscent of the 6th century Arab society. TTP members come mainly from the local tribes, however in some areas; TTP members include some non-Pashtuns from other parts of Pakistan.

In contrast to the radical militant groups, the main agenda of the Tablighi Jamaat is proselytizing to the local tribesmen. Tablighi Jamaat members believe in preaching "pure" Islam to everyone. The Tablighi Jamaat members believe that the Muslims have deviated from the original preaching of the Prophet and his companions. They believe that the only way to eliminate what they view as ills within Muslim society is by purifying the heart and mind of the Muslims.

The local Pashtun tribesmen who support the Tablighi Jamaat appear to have a totally different agenda. They support the Salafists because they get prestige and power in return. In addition, this support to the militants brings badly needed resources—weapons, manpower, explosive expertise, and money—to their families.

Despite all the differences between Salafist groups in the region, their underlying ideology is the same. This ideology, which is anti-Sufism and anti-Shia, is a restricted version of Islam, preaching intolerance and hatred toward non-Salafists. This ideology also supports the use of force to impose what the Tablighi Jamaat views as the "true" tenets of Islam.

This study notes that the tsunami of fundamentalist Salafism has been moving toward the settled districts of

Pakistan. The Salafist move appears to be decentralized, with each tribe or a village having its own local organization with one or more Amirs as its leaders. In the Pashtun inhabited areas of the FATA and Khyber Pakhtunkhwa, the TTP is divided into a series of local vigilante style groups. These groups are autonomous. Examples of this are the Baitullah Mahsud group headed by Wali Ur Rehman, that operates in the Mahsud area of South Waziristan, the Commander Nazir group that operates in the Ahmadzai Wazir area of South Waziristan, the Taliban in North Waziristan headed by Gul Bahadar , the Tariq Afridi group which is active in Dara Adam Khel, the TTP headed by Hakimullah Mahsud, which mainly operates in Kurram and Orakzai. After Baitullah's death, Hakimullah became the leader of TTP, which has Tariq Afridi as its deputy commander.

There are four Taliban groups active in Khyber Agency: Lashkar-i-Islam of Mangal Bagh, Ansarul-i-Islam of Mahbubullah, the Haji Namdar group, and Tamacha (Pistol) Mullah group. In Mohmand Agency, the Abdul Wali and Shah Groups are active. Tehrik Nefaz Sharia Mohammadi (TNSM)[45]

---

[45] Tehreek-e-Nafaz-e-Shariat-e-Mohammadi (TNSM), Movement for the Enforcement of Islamic Law, is a Pakistani militant group whose objective is to enforce Sharia law in Malakand region including Swat, Dir, Chitral, and Bunar. NSNM in 2007 took over much of Swat and Bunar. It was founded by Sufi Muhammad in 1992, and was banned by President Pervez Musharraf on January 12, 2002. The organization is active in the areas along the Pakistan-Afghanistan border. When the founder was imprisoned on January 15, 2002, Maulana Fazlullah, his son-in-law, assumed leadership of the group. Sufi Muhammed was freed in 2008 after he renounced violence, but arrested again when Pakistani military attacked the group in Swat. The military eliminated the TSNM from Swat and Bunar, but the group took refuge in Kunar and Nusristan districts of Afghanistan. In August, the TSNM under the leadership of

headed by Faqir Mohammad and the TSNM headed by Dr. Ismael are active in Bajaur Agency. The TNSM headed by the Fazlullah group and the TNSM headed by Sufi Mohammad are active in Swat valley.

All these groups operate independently, but they operate under a loose confederation called Tehrik Taliban Pakistan (TTP). It is important to note that some groups like Lashkar-e Islam of Mangal Bag and the Commander Nazir Group are not members of the TTP. However, all of these groups claim to be part of the Tablighi Jamaat, a claim the latter has vehemently denied. The underlying ideology of all these groups is Salafism, and they share explosive expertise, manpower, training, money and senior Salafi religious scholars in the region.

These Salafists groups have enforced code of conduct for each tribesman. For example, in Pashtun society, one can't use certain words in a conversation. The phrase "birth control" is not used. "Family planning" is used instead. Instead of saying, "How is your wife?" the locals say "How is your family?" The locals do not congratulate the parents when there is a birth of a baby girl in a family. However, a birth of a boy is celebrated because the birth of a boy enhances a mother's prestige and power in a family.

One of main thrusts of the Taliban and Al-Qa'ida's ideology is to segregate men from women. Any transgression from this rule results in a public execution. In addition, women are not allowed to work outside the home, and in some instances

---

Fazlullah attacked Pakistani military check points in Dir along the border with Afghanistan.

women have been killed because of this. For example, in early 2009 the Taliban killed Malalia Kakar, a famous woman police chief in Kandahar city.[46] Unidentified militants blew up a primary school for girls at Shagai village in Razaar *tehsil* of Swabi District of Khyber Pakhtunkhwa. Ghazala Javed, who sang in her native Pashto language, was gunned down in the northwestern city of Peshawar, along with her father Ghazala Javed.[47] In early May 2009, the Taliban poisoned several girls in Afghanistan on multiple occasions, according to the local and international press.[48]

Interestingly, Islam encourages Muslims to educate their girls, but the Salafists operating along the Pakistan-Afghanistan borderland do not allow girls to get modern education. The Salafist groups enforce rules prohibiting girls from attending modern schools. The Salafists believe that obtaining a modern education has the potential to spread immorality and vulgarity among girls.

The Pashtun Tribes and Salafism

Dozens of Pashtun tribes inhabit Southern and Eastern Afghanistan and Northwestern Pakistan. Millions of Pashtuns also live in Karachi and the Middle East, especially in the Persian Gulf region. The Pashtun tribe is one of the largest tribes in the world, and there are an estimated 50 million Pashtuns worldwide. The most prominent Pashtun tribes are the Yusufzai,

---

[46] http://news.bbc.co.uk/2/hi/7640263.stm
[47] http://www.ibtimes.com/ghazala-javed-victim-talibans-war-women-703384
[48] http://www.huffingtonpost.com/news/afghanistan-war-blog/

Jadoon, Tarin, Mazai, Mada Khel, Daudzai, Marwat, Uthmanzai, Aka Zai, Khalil-Mohamand, Afridi, Mohmand, Tarkani, Uthmanzai, Wazir, Masud, Kakar, Tehir Khel, Bangash, Turi, Achikzai, Khattak, Kundi, Mian Khel, Shinwari, Daur, Safi, Mullagori, Kakar, and two multi-tribal confederations – Durrani and Ghilzai. Each of these Pashtun tribes is further broken down into sub-tribes. The sub-tribes are further divided into clans, which in turn are divided into extended families. The Pashtuns are very religious and traditional in their way of life, and the loyalty found within the extended family system is very strong among the Pashtuns. The senior men make most of the decisions in an extended family and the traditional way of life is passed on from one generation to the next. The family and tribal loyalty are core values in Pashtun culture, and are commonly known as Pashtunwali (see Appendix A for more details).

Pashtun society operates in many layers, where an individual's decision is superseded by his family's decision, a family's decision in turn may be reversed or sustained by a clan's decision, a clan's decision in turn may be questioned by the tribe's decision, and a tribe's decision could be reversed by a multi-tribal decision. A Jirga, a council composed of men with each man representing either himself in case of a family Jirga or a family or a sub-tribe in case of tribal or multi-tribal Jirga, is used as a mechanism to make decisions and enforce them. Pashtun tribal jirga is an assembly of two or more tribesmen who make important decisions including conflict resolution, mediation, and provision of services. The elders in a family arrange all the marriages in the Pashtun culture. All women perform purda (cover their bodies with shawls) when they go out of their homes and socialize only with other women inside their houses, while the men socialize with other men in a mosque or in a hujra, a communal dwelling or a community center where men spend their leisure time in discussions and story-telling to younger members of the village. Traditionally, this was the method used to transfer Pashtunwali from one generation to another along with an effort to preserve their traditional religious views.

Before 1980, the Pashtuns followed a tolerant version of Sunni Islam known as Hanafi Sufi Islam, however an influx of Pashtun workers to the Persian Gulf were exposed to a more radical version of Sunni Islam. As these Pashtun workers returned to Pakistan, they brought this more radical version of Islam back with them, and a gradual change occurred. The emergence of the Mujahideen, a coalition of anti-Soviet insurgents in Afghanistan supported by the US, Saudi Arabia, and Pakistan, along with an influx of Arab jihadists into the Pashtun-controlled area further complicated this change. At this same time, there was an increase in money sent from the Arab states, primarily the wealthy countries in the Gulf region, to Pakistani Deobandi madrassas, where radical clerics preached a more extreme version of Islam, Wahhabism. Finally, the Pakistani government became more tolerant of these radical madaris, and in some cases encouraged, the jihadi groups that radicalized some Pashtuns.

The Taliban have emerged as an enforcer of this Salafi Islam, controlling all aspects of the Pashtun life. A number of Al-Qa'ida members including Osama Bin Laden and Ayman Al-Zawahiri took refuge among these Pashtun tribes and the Taliban harbored Al-Qa'ida members because both groups share same religious Salafi ideology. On May 2, 2011, United States Navy Seals killed Bin Laden in the city of Abbottabad, according to local and international press reports. In return for the tribal support, Al-Qa'ida provides badly needed money, weapons, and manpower to the Taliban since they have been waging a violent insurgency against the US, the NATO forces and the Pakistani military in the Pashtun controlled areas of Pakistan and Afghanistan.

Past literature has reviewed the Pashtun tribes' religious orientation. These Pashtun tribes have a history of fighting with outside invaders after they rally behind a charismatic religious leader while they have shown tolerance when it comes to following Islam. There are major differences between Sufism and Salafism to assist readers in understanding the religious dynamics involved.

This study attempts to explain that in the past the Pashtun tribes were very tolerant in their practice of Islam and followed the Hanafi Sufi School that preached tolerance and accommodation. In their daily practice of their religion, the Pashtun tribesmen have always shown tolerance toward other religions. For example, there were significant number of Sikhs and Hindus living among the Pashtun and the Pashtun nationalist party Khudai Khadmat Gar (Helpers on behalf of God) joined the All India Congress, a Hindu-dominated party in India that opposed the creation of Muslim homeland Pakistan in 1947. Many Salafist-oriented religious leaders view some of the Islamic practices followed by Pashtun tribesmen as un-Islamic or border-line Islamic, but despite this, the Pashtuns would continue to practice those rituals, such as building shrines at the graves of respected Pirs and other religious leaders and primitive rites associated with the shamanistic history of these tribes.

Pashtun Tribal Structure and Salafism

An assertion is made in this study that the Pashtun tribal structure at the sub-tribal level is the key to understanding the "super leadership structure" of Pashtun tribal society. As noted in the previous studies, *Jirga: Pashtun Participatory Governance* and *Jirga: The Way of Pashtun Conflict Resolution*, the changes in the super tribal leadership structure are frequent, and often unexpected. However, the foundation of Pashtun society, the sub-tribal structure, either remains constant or changes very slowly. The balance of power among the families comprising a sub-tribe may change due to numerous factors, including the numerical strength of a family, its financial condition, and access to government positions by the families' leaders, etc., but actual change in the balance of power is either rare or develops very slowly when it does occur. The changes in the super tribal leadership structure, on the other hand, may be swift and occur quite frequently.

There are frequent changes in the super leadership structure of the Pashtun tribal society, with some leaders loosing influence, while others ascend to the leadership positions. Gaining leadership positions in Pashtun society is hard, but retaining leadership positions is even more difficult. A person either inherits or achieves leadership and the leader has to fulfill the local tribe's expectations before he is accepted as the leader or is able to sustain his leadership position. One of the most important requirements of a leader is the ability to mediate between the parties in conflict and this capability defines a leader's level of influence. For example, an elder may be capable of mediating between two brothers in his family, but may lack sufficient stature to mediate between two families within a clan.

An individual may be able to mediate between two families at clan level, but may lack the influence needed to mediate between two clans. Similarly, a leader of a clan may be able to mediate between two clans, but may be unable to mediate between two tribes.

The competition among the leaders, especially among elites at the highest levels of the society is fierce, but is often non-violent. These super elites generally inherit their wealth and economic resources, but some of them acquire the leadership position by acquiring power through actions taken that are perceived to be beneficial to the tribe. However, influence over local tribesmen can be fluid and the leader needs to provide a continuing series of services to the tribesmen, including mediating services or participation in local marriage or funeral rituals to sustain his influence. If he does not provide these services, he may have wealth but he still will have no influence over the tribes.

My previous research and this study show that there is constant competition among the Pashtuns for leadership positions at each level of society. At the sub-tribal level, elders jockey for pre-eminent positions for their families as the elders not only make alliances with the other families within sub-tribes, they also make alliances with dominant elites of the area from the super tribal leadership structure. These elites help the elders expand their influence at the clan level and the elders in return provide the elites with access and influence with the tribesmen in their particular level.

The key to influencing a Pashtun tribe involves the development of an understanding of internal dynamics, and then working with the local family politics at the sub-tribal levels.

Traditionally, "super elites" worked through local elites and these maliks, key leaders appointed to political positions by the government, would manipulate family politics at the sub-tribe level to keep the internal dynamics of a tribe in both balance and under control, according to academic research.[49, 50]

Within the scope of the Tablighi, there is a new breed of Amirs who also use the title "Mullah" who in recent years have bypassed, and in some areas sidelined or killed the elites, maliks, and super-elites to cultivate a direct relationship with the family elders have been manipulating local tribal dynamics to instigate and wage jihad in Pakistan's border region. These violent leaders appear to have emerged from the lower classes of the Pashtun tribes and may have hijacked the Tablighi titles to establish primacy in the tribal and religious hierarchies in which they operate. In addition, another generation of Salafists who are legitimate tribesmen and credible religious leaders also use the title, "Amirs" and they have cultivated direct relationships with the village elders who have direct influence over the local families. One group of these "Amirs" is impatient, violent, and determined to maintain their achieved status by fomenting conflict against the traditional governance systems. The other group seems to be more patient and intent to allow their control over the tribes to be evolutionary rather than revolutionary.

What is striking about this study of the population of Pak Kaya and its vicinity is that there are two major families that

---

[49] Akbar S. Ahmed, *Resistance and Control in Pakistan*. Routledge, London, 2004.
[50] Idris, Khan, *Jirgas: The Pashtun Way of Conflict Resolution*, The Tribal Analysis Center, USA, 2010.

make up the Jehangir Khel sub-tribe and as long as these dominant families were following Sufism, Salafism could not make inroads into the tribe, despite the fact that the Mullah of the local mosque was a Salafist, that a super elite in the region was a prominent Salafi Amir of Tablighi Jamaat, and the Salafi Tablighi groups would frequent the mosque in the village. The fortunes of Tablighi Jamaat, however, changed when a few young men from two elite and dominant families joined the Tablighi Salafi group. The whole village's religious dynamic shifted when as two clearly defined groups emerged, one a Sufi group supported mainly by the elders, and a second Salafi group supported by this young, vocal group. The latter group appears to be gaining strength as the former group appears to weaken over time and as the older, pro-Sufism men die and the younger, pro-Salafi men assume vacant leadership positions in the village.

This contest between the Sufi and the Tablighi Jamaat supporters has been peaceful up to this point, but the competition may take a violent turn if one group tries to force their version of Islam on the other. If this happens, the competition between the two antagonists may turn violent and destabilize the region because any violence between the two groups is likely to draw the neighboring tribes into potential clashes and the whole northern region of Pakistan may descend into open conflict. This has already happened in Pakistan's Khyber Agency where Sufi and Salafi groups had been peaceful competition with one another other for generations, but in the early 2000s, the peaceful contest between two groups turned into open conflicts that were quickly embraced by two sub-tribes within the Afridi Pashtun tribe, the Qambar Khel and Malik Din Khel. Most of the members of the Qambar Khel backed the Salafists while the majority of the Malik Din Khel supported their traditional Sufi beliefs.

Now, the fight that originated as conflict between two sub-tribes has now engulfed almost all the sub-tribes of the entire Afridi tribe. Tribesmen from the Afridi sub-tribes Sepa, Malikdin Khel, Kuki Khel, Zakka Khel, and Aka Khel have joined one group or another and over an extended period of time, both groups have labeled themselves as armed religious movements. The Salafi Afridi group is called Lashkar-i-Islam (Army of Islam) (LI) and is led by Mangal Bag, a Sepha Afridi tribesman. The Sufi group is called Ansar-ul-Islam (Warriors of Islam) (AL), which is headed by a man named Mahbubullah. Both groups are well armed and they have killed dozens of their fellow tribesmen. Occasionally, both groups tried to force the neighboring non-Afridi tribes to support them. For example, Mangal Bag's Lashkar-i-Islam attacked an Adi Khel sub-tribe of the Khalil Mohmand tribe in Peshawar's settled district numerous times over the past few years. The Zakka Khel supported LI, but some LI men killed one of the tribal elders from the Zakka Khel, forcing the tribe to withdraw its support for LI and as of April 2011, the Zakka Khel had shifted its support to the Sufi group, the AL. The Adi Khel sub-tribe was forced to mobilize a lashkar (a tribal war party) to defend themselves and numerous lashkar members have been killed by the Lashkar-i-Islam, including the leader of the Adi Khel Lashkar, Malik Abdul Malik. The Adi Khel and Lashkar-i-Islam have been at war with one another for a few years.

Interestingly, the leaders of the opposing movements in Khyber Agency who originally started the Salafism conflict with the areas Sufis left the area – and they were not even Afridi tribesmen. For example, Pir Saif ur-Rehman was an Afghan and he started Sufism in the Bara sub-district of Khyber Agency before the Pakistani government expelled him and he has been living in one of Pakistan's settled districts. Mufti Munir Shakir, who introduced Salafism into the area, was not an Afridi tribesman, but was a Khattak tribesman from Pakistan's Karak district and he was also expelled from the area, but despite the fact that the two leaders who started the movements didn't remain in Khyber Agency, the fight between the two groups continues. Both groups are joined or supported by AQ, TTP, and other criminal elements and both are heavily armed while the local tribes have joined the fight by supporting either LI or AL.

Fortunately, the Tablighi Jamaat has been very peaceful in Pak Kaya where the competition between the Sufi and the Salafi groups has been peaceful, but like in Khyber Agency, this may change over time. The continuing competition between these two groups may turn into a full-fledged conflict and any initial violent clash in the village may be very destabilizing to the area. An incident in the village may engulf the whole district because there are some prominent, enormous Salafi madrassas are located there, including famous Panjpir Madrassa and Shahmansoor Madrassa. There are thousands of students studying in these two madrassas who come from all over thee Pashtun-inhabited areas in both Afghanistan and Pakistan and their presence may draw the regional tribes into any conflict, potentially creating a civil war between the Sufi tribesmen and the Salafi tribesmen.

The argument may be made that the tribal and family relationship among the Jehangir Khel tribesmen may prevent any violent clashes between two groups, but Pashtun society is structured like an onion where the outer most ring is related to religion, Islam, and a son may fight with his father over religion. This happens in the region. For example, the Ahmadzai Wazirs in South Waziristan mobilized a tribal lashkar again pro-Uzbeks Ahmadzai Wazirs and the tribe split across tribal and family lines. There were three brothers from Yargul Khel sub-tribe of the Zili Khel Ahmadzai tribe, for example, and one brother, Omar, sided with the anti-Uzbek group and two other brothers, Sharif and Noor ul Islam, joined with pro-Uzbek group. In Khyber agency, the Afridi Qambar Khel sub-tribe tribe split into three groups, the Lashkar-i-Islam, Ansar-ul-Islam, and Hajji Namdar group known as Amal Bil Maroof Nahi Anil Munkir. Even some families split and joined three rival groups, Lashkar-i-Islam, Ansar ul-Islam, and Amal Bil Maroof Nahi Anil Munkir. Under the right conditions, this may very well happen in Pak Kaya.

Violence is likely to occur because the local tribesmen have the tendency to mix Pashtunwali, the local Pashtun way of life or local Pashtun "code", and Islam, and the catalyst for a potential battle may very well be the custodianship of the mosque. One group may want to perform certain rituals as dictated by their interpretation of Islam, while the other group may be offended by those rituals. Once an argument starts, this may result in a perceived need to uphold tribal honor. One group may feel that performing these rituals are not only their religious duty, but also part of their tribal honor (Pakhto) and the other group may feel the same way for a different reason. For example, the Sufis normally performed Zakir after each prayer as a part of their Sufi rituals and they argue that they are sending "darudh" (greetings) to Prophet Muhammad. The Salafi group views this as a provocation. Up to now, the Salafi group has turned a blind eye to this objectionable Sufi practice, but this may change as their numerical strength increases. One day, the Salafis may attempt to force the Sufis to stop this provocation while the Sufis, viewing this as part of their honor to exercise their religious duty, may resist Salafist pressure and continue. This competition may very well result in a situation in which religious obligations and tribal honor requires both groups to perform what they may perceive as their rights and plunge the village into open, violent conflict.

There is peace between the two groups in the village now because the split between the Sufi group and the Salafists is across an age line. The parents of the Tablighi Jamaat individuals continue to follow Sufism and in Pashtun culture, children are required to obey their parents and the elders. The Tablighi Amirs appear to be tolerating the provoking behavior of the Sufi group because they are afraid that their parents would side with the Sufi group and that their parents would feel disrespected if they act against the Sufis. As their parents die or convert to Salafism, this last safety net which has been preventing these two groups from violent conflict, may end and trigger open fighting between the two groups. Once fighting starts in the village, surrounding tribes that are also divided between Sufism and Salafism could quickly join one group or the other. This split may provide an opportunity for the radical elements within the Salafists, including TTP and AQ, to join the Salafi group and give the militants a secure foothold about 60 miles from Pakistan's capital, Islamabad. A nearly identical situation occurred for very similar reasons in the Khyber Agency when Afridi sub-tribes joined one religious group or the other.

Background: Kaya and the Utmanzai Tribe

Kaya, a village located on the west bank of Indus River, was located across from the town of Tarbala. Tarbala is now submerged under the lake created in 1974 by the new dam. It was inhabited by two clans of the Yusufzai Utmanzai: the Kanazai and Akazai. Major khels of the Kanazai sub-tribe in Kaya were the Khulam Khel and the Aso Khel. Since the Aso Khel was living with the Kanazai's khels, it was also seen as a section of the Kanazai tribe.

All the tribal elements in the village practiced Sufi Sunni Islam. The Akazai, the largest sub-tribe in the village is divided into a series of tribal elements: the Mani Khel, the Jehangir Khel, the Khudad Khel, and the Sabi Khel. There were two major alliances in Kaya. The Jehangir Khel tribe was aligned with the Khulam Khel and the Behram Khel, and the Khudad Khel was aligned with the Sabi Khel and Aso Khel, which traditionally has enmity against the Jehangir Khel. The Mani Khel was also closer to the Aso Khel, but their traditional enemy was the Khudad Khel. The Sabi Khel was closer to the Khudad Khel because the Sabi Khel and the Jehangir Khel did not get along.

The Jehangir Khel, the subject of this case study, practiced Hanafi Sufi ideology. The major families of the tribe followed the Pir of Ali Sharif, a religious leader from a village Ali Pur in Southern Punjab. The Pir owned a compound on the Indus River's bank where he spent the summer. The local tribes including the Jehangir Khel would provide all the support needed during the Pir's stay in Kabal; a village located three miles from the main village of Kaya. The main families, especially the Hajji and Khabli families that were the most

51

powerful families of the Jehangir Khel, would provide daily rations for the Pir and his disciples. The village's young boys, who were on summer vacation, were encouraged by their parents to stay at the Pir's sprawling compound. The boys' parents encouraged their children to continue to follow the tradition of their ancestors and the boys would perform "baith" (allegiance) to the Pir, a ritual that required the boys to recognize the Pir's sainthood. Please note that in the past some Pashtuns would even give their sons to a Pir as "Nazrana," a religious gift and the Pir would raise the boys as his "challas," disciples, however this practice no longer takes place since there has been an increasing trend, especially among the poor, to send their sons to madrassas where they will get a free religious education along with food and lodging.

Pir Ali Sharif provided some religious services to the tribesmen by praying for the well-being of the tribes and for the ills that could visit them. The Pir would pray for the prosperity of the tribesmen, but he would not mingle with the people in order to maintain the image of personal uniqueness. In addition, he would also give everyone "Taiweez", a few Quranic verses written on a piece of paper which a tribesman would stitch into leather pouch and wear around his neck as an amulet.

The Pir was viewed as very bureaucratic and extremely elite in his lifestyle. For example, he would not eat with the tribesmen and he would not share his crockery with the tribesmen because he was afraid that he might catch diseases from them. The Pir didn't encourage the tribesmen to send their children to school in order to ensure a constant supply of disciples remaining under his control. Additionally, he was observed to pray only during the afternoon and evening prayers and he was not observed to wake up early in the morning to pray with the locals, instead sleeping until 10 am.

There were numerous rumors and stories around the area about the Pir that would give him more religious and social standing among the tribesmen. For example, the Hajji family followed the Pir because Hajji Azim Khan, the patriarch of the family and a prominent leader of the Jehangir Khel, spread a rumor that his "baith" to the Pir resulted in his prosperity. In order to maintain the support of his immediate family in a dispute with his step-brothers, he would tell his sons and grandsons that he was the only son from his father's first wife and that his step brothers, who were more powerful at the time than he was, would not give him a fair share in his father's inheritance. Azim Khan said he went to Ali Sharif and performed "baith" to the father of the current Pir Ali Shah. After Azim Khan's "baith," God brought prosperity and wealth to him and to his family. He believed that God bestowed him with more land than his brothers due to this "baith." Azim Khan said he was blessed with hajj, a once in lifetime visit to Mecca and Medina in Saudi Arabia, due to this wealth. In addition, he was the only man in his tribe who could afford to send his four sons on the hajj in 1960s. Azim Khan said he used his wealth to buy more land. Due to his "baith" to the Pir, he became wealthier than his brothers. His sons and grandsons believed in his stories and followed his tradition. As a result, all of his sons and grandsons performed "baith" to the Pir.

In the early 1970s, the government of Pakistan built the Tarbala dam which submerged the original Kaya-Kabal villages. The Jehangir Khel was forced to migrate to Swabi district, about 15 miles south of the Tarbala Dam, but the Pir, who would spend summers in Kaya-Kabal, did not build a house in the new village of Pak-Kaya. However, the Pir was seen visiting the new village periodically where the tribesmen would take turns providing big feasts and lodge the Pir and his entourage.

Pak Kaya

The Jehangir Khel tribesmen and some of their allies settled in Swabi District and named this new settlement Pak Kaya, or "Pure Kaya". Pak Kaya village is situated on the west bank of the Indus River near a historical village, Hund, where Alexander the Great once stayed before he invaded India. Pak Kaya village is divided into two small sections: Bar Kaya and Qoz Kaya. This study focuses on the Jehangir Khel tribe which inhabits Qoz Kaya.

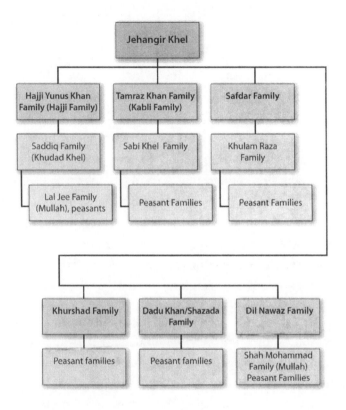

Figure 3. Leading Families of the Jehangir Khel.

The total population of both villages is about 1000, with about 250 to 300 households. The main livelihood in the village is agriculture, but there are some young men working in the Middle East, Japan, Korea, the United States, and the United Kingdom who send remittances to their families. Both villages are relatively prosperous when compared to the surrounding villages, which you can clearly see because all the houses in the village are made of cement, the streets are paved, and there are elementary and high schools for boys and a secondary school for girls. There was shortage of labor in the village during the green

55

bean harvest in March 2010, and the local landowners have complained that there is a shortage of agriculture labor, in general, suggesting that most of the tribesmen are currently employed in other ways. A local landlord on 5 March 2010 noted that some emigrant families from Bajaur and Mohmand Agencies in the FATA, as well as families from Afghanistan, settled in the village as peasant sharecroppers after violence began in their home regions and forced them to leave to seek safety. The landlord added that arriving families were given free housing by the landowners and in return, these families work on the farms as sharecroppers. Like other Pashtun areas, the literacy rate is very low among the peasants and among the poor segment of the society, while the education level is relatively high among the more prosperous Pashtun landowners.

In addition to income from agriculture and remittances from abroad, some families' income comes from the trucking business, trading, and small businesses. This increased infusion of money into the area has inflated the price of local land in recent years, further enhancing the power and the prestige of the Pashtun landowners.

The Qoz Kaya portion of Pak Kaya is inhabited mainly by the Jehangir Khel Pashtuns, a sub-tribe of the Akazai, which is a sub-tribe of Uthmanzai, which in turn is a sub-tribe of the Yusufzai Pashtuns. There are some Pashtun families from other tribes who are related to the key families of the Jehangir Khel and who also live in the village (*see* Figure 3). For example, there are families from the Sabi Khel, Mani Khel, and Khudad Khel, three sub-tribes of Akazai Utmanzai Yusufzai sub-tribe. In addition to these families, there are numerous other families that are viewed as dependent families living with the Pashtuns and performing functions the Pashtuns are unable, or unwilling, to do for themselves. These include the two mullahs' families, a barber's family, one blacksmith family, a weaver's family, and a few Gujar families. Most of the dependent families live in houses belonging to the Pashtun land-owning families. Importantly, the village's land is only owned by Pashtun families.

Major decisions are made in the village's jirga, which includes a senior male member of each Pashtun family and the two mullahs' families. The dependent families are not invited to the village jirgas unless a dependent family is a party to a dispute or unless a jirga is convened to deal with a matter related to a dependent family member. The two mullahs' families have been living with the Jehangir Khel tribe for generations and despite the fact that there are no intermarriages between the Pashtun families and the Mullahs' families, the latter are respected and are invited to attend tribal Jirgas.

The Jehangir Khel in the village is divided into six major families (*see* Figure 3). These include the Hajji family, the Khabli family, the Khurshad family, the Dil Nawaz Family, the Dost Mohammad Family, and the Safder Khan family. The most powerful families are the Hajji, Khabli and Safder families. The other families have aligned themselves with these powerful families to create three major blocs within the Jehangir Khel tribe and there is constant tension among the three major families over small, petty issues, including water distribution and land demarcation. The rest of the village families, including the non-Jehangir Khel Pashtun, have aligned themselves with the three major Jehangir Khel families to protect their own interests. For example, Karam Khan from the Mani Khel family has aligned himself with Dil Nawaz's family. Saddiq Khan's family of the Khudad Khel allied itself with the Hajji family and the Safder family and the Sabi Khel family is connected to the Khabli family. The peasants and Gujars support their landlords from the Pashtun families.

This study determined that the single most important factor that brings different Pashtun families together to help shape an alliance involved intermarriage. For example, the Hajji Family has an extended network within the Jehangir Khel and beyond because of intermarriages. The Hajji Family is related to almost all the families of the Jehangir Khel. The late Hajji Azim Khan had four sons and the eldest son, Yunus Khan, married into Dadu Khan's family. Daud Khan, the second son, married into the Khabli family and Ayub Khan, the third son, married into Safdar Khan's family. Sulaman Khan, the youngest son, married into Dil Nawaz's family. Finally, Azim Khan's two daughters married into the Khalil Khan and Chaman Khan families to form alliances that used to be common in medieval Europe.

Unlike in the west, within Pashtun society, the maternal relationship is more important than the paternal relationship because in Pashtun tribes land ownership and leadership is inherited through paternal relationship, causing jealousy and disputes, especially within the male paternal cousins who have equal claims to their grandfather's land. The cousins from the maternal relationship tend to be very close and call themselves "Masara" or "Mom's relatives", whereas the cousins from the paternal relationship are called "tarboor" or "competitors" and this competition is identified as "taborwali," or cousin enmity. The Pashtun notion of uncle is different than in other societies and uncles from the paternal side are called "toroh" while the uncles from the maternal side are called "mama," which carries much more closeness and bonds. The children of two sisters, known as "Masaras," tend to be very close. However, the children of two brothers can become enemies due to disputes over land inheritance and jealousy.

Tribesmen and the Myths about the Pirs

After the Jehangir Khel tribesmen migrated to Pak-Kaya, a few Pirs started visiting the village. Three Pirs in particular Pir Ali Shah, Challa Badshah, also called the Chlla Bajee, or "Lunatic Pir), and Jalbai Pir, became regular visitors in the village.

Pir Jamaat Ali Shah's family was originally from Alipur, Punjab and the family built a compound in old Kaya-Kabal village. After Pir Jamaat Ali's death in 1951, his son Pir Mehar Ali Shah became the Gadi Nesheeen, the custodian. The Jehangir Khel tribesmen were the disciples of this Pir and all the tribesmen performed "baith" to the Pir, vowing to accept the Pir's sainthood and his religious authority. The Jehangir Khel tribe also provided material support for the Pir when he would spend the summer in Kaya-Kabal.

A Brief Background of Pir Jamaat Ali Shah

Pir Sayyad Jamaat Ali Shah Naqshbandi-Mujaddidi (1840 -1951) lived in Alipur Sharif, Sialkot, Pakistan. The Pir's ancestors originated from Shiraz, Persia, and came to the subcontinent with the Mugal Emperor Humayoun when he returned to Delhi after his exile in Iran, when Mugal Emperor Akbar announced his "Din i Ilaahi." Akbar introduced Din-i-Ilaahi, consisting of some tenets and practices from both Islam and the Hindu religion to pacify the majority Hindu population and to create unity between Muslims and Hindus in India. Some senior Muslim religious leaders viewed Akbar's act as un-Islamic and rebelled against the regime. The Pir's family left the imperial court in protest and Akbar gave the Pir's family land in the Alipur area. Jamaat Ali Shah completed his religious education and laid the foundation stones for his mosque and funded hundreds of other mosques, from Peshawar to Hyderabad, Deccan, in India. He also participated in the Khilafat Movement, a protest campaign intended to protect the Ottoman Empire following World War I, and the Arya Samaj Movement, a Hindu reform campaign. He was a defender of the Ahl as-Sunnah faith against the rise of Qadianism, or the Ahmadiyya Movement that was considered apostate by other Muslims, and the Wahabbis. He was estimated to have over 1 million murids, or disciples, in a region from Afghanistan to the southern tip of India. He was a supporter of the Pakistan movement and issued a fatwa saying that he would not read the janazah prayer, or funeral, for any of his murid who did not vote for Pakistan.[51] After Jamaat Ali Shah's death, Pir Mehar Ali Shah became the Pir and recently, Pir Tefsir Ali Shah, the son of Mehar Ali Shah, took over as Pir in the region.

---

[51] http://www.yanabi.com/forum/Topic208406-32-1.aspx.

The Pir's influence spread across all the Jehangir Khel's families. There were a significant number of the local tribesmen who believed the following stories and myths about these Pirs:

1. In the 19th century, there was a debate between a Wahhabi cleric and Pir Jamaat Ali Shah, the patriarch of the Pir family. The Wahhabi Mullah did not believe that prophet Muhammad was "noor" (spirit). After a long inconclusive debate, Pir Jamaat Ali Shah challenged the Wahhabi cleric for a walk on hot coals and the Pir argued that the fire would not hurt the one who was right. The Wahhabi Mullah declined the challenge, the Pir walked on the coals, which did not hurt the Pir, proving his sainthood.

2. The Pir's "Langure", the cooking area where free food was served to everyone, was never depleted because there is a "barkat", or God's blessing, in the food and one bushel of rice fed hundreds of people. If a tribesman donated a goat, cow, or a bushel of wheat or corn, or a bucket of milk his resources or his herds would multiply through the Pir's blessing.

3. The Pir's blessing and prayer could cure any disease. If a sick tribesman ate "khurda", the food at Pir's compound, he would be cured due to the "khurda" being blessed by the Pir's prayers. "Khurda" also cured the disabled.

4. If a tribesman stole anything from the Pir's compound, hurt the Pir, or tried to hurt the Pir or his murid, or "challas" (devotees or disciples), he would be hurt both physically and materially. The tribesman's descendants would be born with disabilities if he indulges in anti-Pir activities.

5. A tribesman donating land, "seerai", to the Pir would be blessed by God with prosperity and richness for this donation to the Pir.

6. The Pir served as a middleman between the Prophet Muhammad and God. The Pir would certify on the Day of Judgment to God and the Prophet that a tribesman is a righteous man and should go to the Heaven.

7. The Pirs prayed for women who are unable to bear sons. He also gave amulets for women to wear which help them give birth to sons.

8. Some women with "mirgai," or epilepsy, go to the Pir who would give them amulets and pray for the women. The tribesmen believed that the Pir's prayers and amulets would help cure the women.

Pir Challa Badshah (the Crazy or Lunatic King)

Challa Badshah was originally from a small village called Seeri, located about three miles north of old Kaya near Tarbala. The Nawab of Amb, the local ruler of Amb state, gave him land near Shergarh in Manserah district as a "seerai" or gift. Challa built a small settlement where he would spend the summer along with his disciples. Challa Pir followed Pir Shah Baz Mas Qalandar, a famous Sufi Pir in Sindh, Pakistan, whose mausoleum attracts millions of people every year to the city of Savan in Sindh. Challa Pir went to Karachi and illegally occupied a piece of land on the main Indus highway where he built a small settlement consisting of a few mud structures. There are a large number of Pashtuns in Karachi who donate money to the Pir and he opened free living quarters and a langare for everyone at the site. Unlike Pir Ali Shah, Challa

Badshah would not pray as required by Islam. He also smoked an extensive amount of hashish and every murid, in his company would indulge in heavy hashish smoking and dancing. The Challa and his murids would indulge in smoking hashish and dancing every night

Challa Badshah did not live in Pak Kaya, but he would visit once in a while. A Jehangir Khel tribesman, Dos Mohammad Khan, donated about 1/8 of an acre to Challa on the bank of Badrai River, but Challa Badshah has not built his camp there. There were numerous rumors and myths associated with this Pir and his family.

1. In the past, Challa Badshah walked on fire. The fire did not hurt him, proving he is a saint.
2. Challa Badshah did not need to pray as required by other Muslims because he was a direct descendent of the Prophet Muhammad. Regardless of the religious transgression he was involved in, Challa Badshah was immune from any punishment by Allah because he was an "Allah wala", a selected man of Allah who has given him special permission to transgress.
3. Anyone arguing or using insulting language against Challa was punished by hidden forces of Allah. Anybody who disobeyed him was also punished by the hidden forces of Allah. If a tribesman was involved in any transgression against Challa, he would be punished by hidden forces of Allah and the tribesman and his family become disabled. The financial well-being of the tribesman would be ruined.

4. Hashish smoking and dancing rituals were acceptable because Challa is special and Allah did not oblige him to fulfill all the duties of Islam. Challa was immune to performing any duty obligated by the Allah because he was "Allah wala" (Allah's special person).

Interestingly, almost all the Jehangir Khel tribesmen believed in all these rumors and stories and the tribesmen would respect the Pir when he would come to visit. They would kiss his hand when they would meet with him and would bend when they shook hands with the Pir as a show of subservience. It was interesting to note that the Pir did not accumulate wealth or money. The tribesmen would bring him basic necessities and food cooked by his disciples. Hashish was also donated and freely available to every smoker. Free tobacco was also available since the tribesmen donated all these products to the langare.

In contrast, Pir Ali Shah was a rich man who owned lot of land in Punjab. He also received a large sum of money as compensation from the government when his property in old Kaya-Kabal was damaged due to the Tarbala Dam's flooding. Pir Ali Shah also required services when he visited and the tribesmen would make big feasts for the Pir when he came to visit Pak-Kaya. The Pir's bed was decorated with all new cloth and pillows. In contrast, Challa Badshah was very down to earth. He would eat very simple food. Challa would eat food with the tribesmen while Pir Ali Shah would eat separately. Pir Ali Shah would even carry his own crockery. In contrast, Challa was the people's Pir. He would eat, sleep, and dine with the people on floor.

The Jalbai Pir:

The Jalbai Pir was from a small village, Jalbai, located about 10 miles from Pak Kaya. The Pir's family is very famous in the area and the author observed the Pir, complete with his nail fungus, during the Pir's visit to the village in May 2010. He grew his nails very long and there is a rumor associated with the nails and his nail fungus. According to the local legend, both the Pir and his brother had special nails that are unique and holy. Allah gave these brothers special nails as a sign that they are Allah's special human beings. When the Pir visited the village, the tribesmen especially Khalil Khan, a prominent elder, and Mohammad Ayub Khan, the elder from the Hajji family, would host him. The tribesmen were observed to prepare a special feast for the Pir, but the influence of the Pir was restricted to only few families.

1. The special nails of the two brothers are evidence that they are saints and those two brothers are the Allah's "noor" (spirit).

2. The Pir's prayers cured the disabled and the ill. Tribesmen with disability or illness were seen visiting the house of the Pir's family where the Pir would pray for the visitors and would give amulets.

3. The Pir's family received special "Ajazat", or permission, to cure people who are bitten by snakes. The Pir would use his prayers and miracles to remove the poison from the body of snake-stricken tribesman.

4. Some women would have "mirgai" (epilepsy) and they would go to the Pir who would give them amulets and pray for the women. The tribesmen

believed that the Pir's prayers and amulets would help cure the women.

Unlike Challa Pir, this Pir was not observed smoking Hashish or tobacco. The Pir was also observed to pray five times a day. Unlike Pir Ali Shah, the Pir did not require a large amount of support. The Pir was observed to eat with his hosts and he was also not a wealthy landowner. Unlike both Challa and Pir Ali Shah, the Jalbai Pir did not have an open langare. The tribesmen were observed to visit the Pir and would leave without any entertainment and would voluntarily donate money that was used by the Pir's family to support them.

Social and Economic Structure of the Village

As noted previously, the Jehangir Khel, a sub-tribe of the Utmanzai Yusufzai tribe, is the dominant tribe in Pak Kaya village. There are several families from the Mani Khel, Aso Khel, Musa Khel sub-tribes of the Utmanzai tribe and these families are recognized as Pashtun families because they own land. The sizes of the land holdings vary from family to family. It was interesting to learn that land holding did not define a family's influence in the village. Instead, the size of the family and its network defines its power and influence. For example, the Khabli family is very powerful, but the family's landholding is much smaller than other dominant families. The size of the landholding ranges from a couple of acres to 100 acres depending on the family.

As discussed previously, in addition to Pashtun families, there are several families from Afghanistan and other areas of the FATA that live with the tribesmen as peasants who are provided free housing by the tribesmen. These include the families of a drummer, a weaver, a blacksmith, and a barber. In addition, there are the families of two Mullahs, and two Sahabzada families who are also viewed as dependent families.

Each family is invited to attend regular village jirgas called to address issues such as marriage, death, cleaning of mosque or a "hujra", or cleaning water canals. Only Pashtun families are invited to important jirgas dealing with security issues, but dependent families can participate if they are involved in a dispute. Since the jirgas are held in the open, young Pashtun men and the men from the dependent classes can sit and observe the proceedings.

Agriculture is a main livelihood in the village. There are some men who work overseas, especially in Japan, Korea, the United Kingdom, and the Middle East, who send remittances back to their families. The peasants work the land on a sharecropping basis and generally the land owners provide free housing, seed and fertilizer while the peasants provide the labor. The agriculture proceeds are split equally between the landowners and the peasants. The tribesmen grow mainly green beans, sugarcane, corn, wheat, and tobacco. They used to grow opium, but in 1979 the Pakistani government banned opium cultivation. The tribesmen complained that this transition from a cash crop like opium to other crops was difficult, but they managed to replace opium with other cash crops.

Women and Salafism

The Pashtuns in general and the Jehangir Khel in particular, are very conservative and restrictive when it comes to women and their roles in the society. Women are not allowed to work outside the home or go shopping without having a male relative along with her as an escort. The women work at home and are involved in a series of activities inside their homes. For example, women care for the livestock, clean and cook three meals a day and since many of the villagers lack refrigerators, this process is made much more arduous.

As in many areas in Pakistan, there is an arranged marriage system in the villages. In addition, a significant number of girls are married to their cousins, but in recent years, a few girls were married to men from outside the tribe. It is customary that a bride's family provides all household items, including furniture, pots, crockery, a refrigerator if it can be afforded, and a cooler for the new family's use. The groom's family provides quilts and beds. It is common to see multiple related families living in a same compound owned by the senior male in the extended family.

Before Salafism was introduced, women would watch television in their spare time. In addition, while men and women would have separate parties during marriage ceremonies, women would invite drummers and arrange a dance party for their entertainment on these special occasions.

In recent years, as Tablighi Jamaat increased their control over the village, television was banned inside houses where the women had previously watched it, and women could not enjoy music and dance at marriage ceremonies. In addition, the puritanical Tablighi Jamaat prohibited music and other entertainment in the village and hujra.

Traditionally, the women covered themselves, from head to toe when they left their homes, but in recent years, some women have started wearing the black abaya commonly seen in the Middle East. None of the women in the village were observed wearing the Afghan-style burqa.

The educational level among women is very low, although there is a girls' elementary school in the village. Some of the girls were seen going to the school, but most do not continue their education after elementary school. A couple of girls were observed going to a nearby village to attend middle school, but there is not a single female living in the village who attends college. The village tribesmen strongly believe in the Pashtun proverb that suggests there are only two places for a woman: the "Core" and the "Gore", or the house and the graveyard.

The members of Tablighi Jamaat in the village are educated and most have attended college. Some even have non-agricultural jobs. Despite their exposure to modern institutions, Tablighis remain very conservative when it comes to women, and instead of easing restrictions on the village women, the Tablighis place even more restrictions on them. Salafists strongly believe and practice gender segregation in the village, but they are not necessarily against women's education. However, they oppose co-education for girls and boys and they clearly object to women working outside the home. Interestingly, the Tablighis were observed sending their female relatives to preach their message to other women.

The Salafist and Tablighi Jamaat's restrictive practices toward women are consistent with Pashtun culture and are quickly accepted. Tablighi Jamaat's preaching to the tribesmen about women and their role in society appeals to the locals since Pashtun social values in general are very close to what the Tablighi Jamaat preaches. In Pashtun society, it is nearly impossible for an unrelated man and a woman, no matter how educated or modern, to talk with each other, even on the phone. Men and women live in social and cultural shells that are impossible to break, and despite modern education, urbanization, and modern communication, these traditional shells remain strong and durable. Men and women have no chance to socialize together since there are so many barriers that inhibit their ability to socialize. These barriers are created by local social and cultural values, and the way these values are enforced clearly favor men over women, and perpetuate male dominance over women. These values seemed to be impossible to break because there are so many guardians, including the average man and the Taliban. As a result of the social and cultural pressures on them, most young people have no choice but to accept arranged marriages. A marriage among the Pashtuns is viewed as providing social and economic security, especially for women, and the children resulting from a marriage are a major source of security for parents in their old age.

There are numerous checks and fears ingrained in the Pashtun system that favor militants. These checks and constraints are more severe for young, unmarried females who live in an environment of fear. A young Pashtun girl always fears her brothers, parents, relatives, friends, and the men around her. No matter how educated she might be this fear remains the part of a female's personality, even to the point where she is

70

afraid to talk on the phone because of this deeply ingrained fear. It becomes impossible for a woman to talk to a man and a man can't visit a woman's house or take her on a date since women are haunted by the fear of the unknown that is created by the dangerous socialization process in Pashtun society. Additionally, there is a fear of the Taliban who play a role of social "Minutemen" for Pashtun society. They police Pashtun culture with most extreme version of Islam that is then imposed on the locals.

The socially rigid Taliban, for example, do not allow men to shave their beards and women are not allowed to leave their homes without the company of a male relative. The Taliban do not allow music or TV and they don't even allow girls to go to school.

The way females are taught in Pashtun society has something to do with their fear. Females are conditioned to be submissive, obedient, shy and dependent first on their parents and brothers, then on their husbands. This increasing dependency inhibits their ability to make independent decisions, and develop confident personalities. Most young girls don't even dream about becoming independent from their families.

In Pashtun culture, the issue of marriage cannot be separated from the issue of the relationship between a man and a woman. Most of the females in the Pashtun society believe that relationships must logically conclude in marriage and that the concept of a friendship or an affair is impossible to think of without marriage.

A "code of conduct" for women was created by the men in Pashtun society, and is passed down from one generation to the next and when it comes to enforcement, every man becomes a vigilante. In recent days, the Taliban have become the "enforcers-in-chief" of the local culture and its values and in certain cases, even the general public gets involved. Women are forced to obey this code of conduct whether they approve of it or not. They cannot change these cultural restrictions because rebellion results in being labeled as "modern," which in turn results in a social death. There is not a single political movement or party that voices concern over the cruel and inhuman treatment of the women in Pashtun society. Modern education, urbanization, and communication have also failed to change the situation that weighs so heavily on Pashtun women. Instead, these relatively new social forces have perpetuated traditional cultural restrictions. Women have no choice but to subject themselves to these restrictions due to social and economic pressures and since the women in the Pashtun society are so dependent upon men, it is impossible to break free. Most women want to get out of this cruel and inhuman situation, but they can't escape because of social and cultural pressure. In addition, men have a stake in maintaining these restrictions on women, while simultaneously framing complete different standards for themselves. Pashtun women are left with no choice but to follow something that they prefer to avoid.

Unlike western society in which a woman meets and openly dates a man, in Pashtun society, women can't follow this simple social process. The concept of a date is out of question in Pashtun society where no one dares to be seen with a member of the opposite sex before marriage. Women adhere to these conditions because they are afraid of being labeled as morally corrupt within their community. Once this label is attached to a young girl, it can ruin her chance of ever marrying into a respectable family and her alleged behavior can also bring a bad name to her entire family, undermining their power and prestige in the society. It is interesting to see how this entire drama is played out because once a young woman is labeled "corrupt" she loses her social standing and becomes an outcast. It is also interesting to see the impact of this corruptness label. Some people consider a modern women working in an office or one who does not cover herself completely when outside the home to be socially corrupt. Even talking on the phone with a person of the opposite sex is viewed as being morally and socially corrupt. For a woman, talking on the phone to someone who is not a close relative is considered an act of immorality, but these labels do not apply equally to men.

Within the Islamic religion, men can marry any Muslim (including a Sayed), Jew, or Christian. However, there is a tradition among the Pashtuns that a Pashtun man is not allowed to marry within a Sayed family. Some people believe that marrying a Sayed woman is un-Islamic because these women are special and regarded as holy because they are descendants of Prophet Muhammad. Some Pashtuns believe that if a non-Sayed marries a Sayed woman, either the husband or the wife will die, or something will happen to their children. These old superstitious beliefs are hard to break. Interestingly, and like many marriage choices available to Pashtun males, a Sayed man may marry a non-Sayed woman. Again, it is not the Islamic religion that prohibits a non-Sayed man from marrying a Sayed woman; rather it is local Pashtun tradition, something that the Tablighi Jamaat opposes. They believe that any Muslim man can marry any Muslim woman.

The Tablighi Jamaat members don't accept the concept of romance or dating before marriage, something that is consistent with Pashtun culture. In the Pashtun society, the concept of love is remote when it comes to marriage and hardly anybody considers love to be an important foundation for a marriage. Rather, most of the people have a firm belief that the marriages based on love have more problems than the marriages without it. Additionally, most people end up marrying someone within their extended families. If there is a marriage with someone outside the family, the economic and political position of the new family connection is an important consideration because social and economic security is derived from a marriage to someone from a rich and politically powerful family.

For a woman, social and economic security is more important given her position within the male dominant society and it is important to understand how social security for women is passed on from one generation to another. First, parents provide social security, but this is passed on to brothers as parents grow older and eventually die. Later, the social and economic responsibility for the woman is handed over to a husband. Most people take into account the economic dimension of marriage rather than the emotional component. Few people consider love an important factor in the marriage. Rather, a person's family, level of income, level of education, and the family's political influence are all considered more important.

Unlike western society where love is considered the major reason to marry someone and a lessening of love is a good reason to get out of it, in Pashtun society nobody seems to pay attention to love in spite of the fact that Pashtun poetry and music consists of lyrics full of love, indulgence in drinking and

74

the use of hashish. Pashtun poets and musicians express rebellion from this oppressive culture and religious values. The loveless marriage concept is consistent with the views of the Tablighi Jamaat that considers love to be irrational. Tablighis argue that love reflects emotions rather than reason and that reason, not emotion, should be the basis for marriage. Most Pashtuns believe that social and economic factors such as family education, status, and political background are a more rational basis for marriage.

Pashtun Tribes: Drivers of Change from Sufism to Salafism

There appear to be numerous drivers of social and religious change among the Pashtun tribes that are shifting from the traditional tribal social order to the new Salafi social and religious orientation. Modern education, communication and proximity to the major cities of Peshawar, Mardan, Nowshera, Islamabad and Rawalpindi, immigration, and an influx of remittances into villages have brought increasing prosperity that is changing the tribesmen's beliefs and social orientation.

Contrary to what is predicted by modernization theorists, the modern institutions noted above have been orienting the local Pashtuns to Salafism. Instead of making the Pashtuns more liberal and secular, the modern institutions, such as modern education, exposure to city life and jobs in the modern economy are converting the Pashtuns in the village into Salafists who follow a more restrictive version of Sunni Islam.

In old Kaya, there was not a single college graduate among the Jehangir Khel tribesmen and there were only a couple of high school graduates in the tribe. Old Kaya was not connected with the rest of the world by road or a telephone and there was no electricity or running water. It would take a half-day to travel by foot to Tarbala village and this trip involved a boat journey across the Indus River. In summer, this trip was even more difficult due to the usual surge of water in the Indus River. There was a primary school where a student could get up to eight years of education, but the quality of the teachers was very bad and students had to travel to Tarbala to get a high school diploma.

The villagers in old Kaya were religious, but they followed Sufism, a liberal, tolerant version of Sunni Islam. There was not a single Salafist in the village and as noted earlier, the tribesmen followed a tolerant version of Sufism.

In old Kaya village there was no electricity and the locals would use wood for cooking. There was no phone service, and the nearest phone center was in Tarbala town, which was a half-day away.

In early 1970s, after the Tarbela Dam was completed, the tribesmen migrated to Pak Kaya in Swabi. By 2010, there was running water in the village along with electricity and telephone service and cell phone and dial-up Internet service was available. In addition, there are primary and high schools in the village or nearby in Hund. The tribesmen have access to satellite television and radios. Unlike in the old Kaya village where there was hardly a cement house, in the current village of Pak Kaya almost all the houses are made of cement.

There is paved road access to the village from the main highway and a tribesman can travel to the major cities of

Peshawar and Islamabad in an hour. The paved road means quick access to the market and the tribesmen grow vegetables, wheat and corn, which they quickly market in the major cities, bringing in revenue to the village. The streets of the village are paved and there is even underground sewage in a few streets. In old Kaya, nobody had a toilet facility. In contrast, most of the houses in the village now have a toilet facility. In old Kaya, not a single tribesman owned a car. In the new Pak Kaya, some families own cars and trucks.

Numerous young men left the village and migrated to the Middle East, the United Kingdom, Japan, Korea, and the United States, and these young men have been remitting money and new ideas back to the village. The influx of money and new ideas has been the source of much of the transformation of the local social and religious orientation of the village.

It is interesting to note that this influx of remittances and new ideas has not changed the local tribal structure. Tribal decisions continue to be made by a jirga made up of the major Jehangir Khel families. The jirga remains a main mechanism for all decisions. Despite all the changes in the village due the factors noted above, the local Pashtun tribal structure remains unchanged. The three families – Hajji, Khabli, and Safdar – remain influential within the tribal dynamics and in the jirga decision-making process.

What has changed is the inroad by Salafism through the Tablighi Jamaat. In the early 2000's, there was not a single Salafi or Tablighi member other than a Mullah in the village. Now, almost half the village follows Tablighi Jamaat's ideology. Additionally, there are two active Amirs of the Tablighi Jamaat in the tribe and since both Amirs come from the powerful Hajji and Khabli families, they are able to openly challenge the people who continue to practice Sufism.

Education remains a key driver in this religious change in the tribe. A common belief is that modern education liberalizes a population, but in the village modern education appears to cause a change in religious orientation from Sufism to Salafism. In this case, modern education appears to make young men more religious and conservative in their political views. The young men from the Hajji and Khabli families who pioneered the introduction of Salafism in the village were college graduates and one even lived in the United Kingdom for several years. Both young men had been liberal in their orientation before they joined the Tablighi Jamaat, but both young men were converted into Tablighi Jamaat when they were students at the university in Peshawar and they introduced Tablighi Jamaat to the village. With the conversion of these two tribesmen, the local Mullah who had been a Deobandi became active and began to openly preach the Tablighi Jamaat's ideology.

In addition to the two Amirs, almost all the members of the Tablighi Jamaat were young men and college graduates under the age 30. Other than the Mullah, not a single member of Tablighi Jamaat was over 40 years old and in most of the families, the younger members became members of the Tablighi Jamaat while the older family members remained followers of Sufism and the Pirs.

Tribal Fissures and the Emerging Strain of Salafism

As explained previously, the Pashtun tribal structure at the local clan or sub-tribe level has remained unchanged despite an increase in educational levels, improvements in communications, access to city markets leading to increased economic prosperity, an infusion of remittances from abroad, and the arrival of new ideas. These drivers of change appear to have altered the religious outlook of the tribesmen from more the traditionally liberal Sufism to the more restrictive Salafism that is practiced outside of South Asia.

A closer look at the social change reveals shifts from the traditional Sufi Islamic practices to this new Salafi Tablighi Jamaat practice has created divisions within the families that make up the Jehangir Khel tribe, at least for now. Oddly, at the same time this new Salafism is also bridging the divide among the local families that make up a Pashtun tribe and initially, at least, appears to be bringing stability to the area.

Traditionally, a Pashtun family would remain united on nearly any issue and would always be expected to support its members. Furthermore, a family elder would present the family's position on an issue to the rest of the families at the tribal level through the jirga system and the elder would get feedback from other family members before making a final decision on behalf of his family. Within the family, however, there was always tension among brothers or cousins present over inheritance of property, water distribution, or interfamily marriage issues. However, the shift from the Sufi Islamic orientation to Salafi Tablighi has been creating fissures within the families that had nothing to do with traditional, Pashtunwali-based tensions. These divisions within families that were created over the sensitive issue of religion gradually may erode the family structure, a main source of stability in the Pashtun society, as the older generation tends to follow the traditions within Sufism while their younger relatives are more receptive to the changes suggested by the "missionary" Amirs. In addition, the Amirs within an elite family are likely to replace the traditional family elders who ensured peace and stability. In contrast to the consensus style of the older generation's elders, the young Amirs are likely to be prone to the use of force and violence as a means to force change upon the tribes.

This change within the family structure may continue to erode the Pashtun tribal structure that has been critical in maintaining stability at the village level. The local tribal structure has played a critical role in maintaining order, security, and stability in Pashtun communities, with the elders of the families maintaining a degree of stability through the use of the jirga process at the sub-tribe level. With the erosion of the elders' influence within the families, this rapidly developing process could end the safety net that has held Pashtun society together. The elders, who were the part of the traditional tribal structure, keep their families aligned with the traditional elites in the area who provide political, economic and social protection to allow the elders to operate at the village level. Erosion of the elders' influence and the ascendance of the young Salafi Amirs is likely to realign the whole leadership structure and along with that shifting of power, the decision-making process. The Amirs are likely to align their families with the religious figures in the area rather than with the elites, who they view as corrupt and irreligious, further eroding the influence of the traditional elites, and enhancing the influence and power of the Salafi religious establishment.

One example can be seen with the Hajji family that was always united when it came to following Sufi Islam. The family was the first one in the village to commit baith to Pir Ali Shah and every member of the family became a murid of Pir Ali Shah and the patriarch of the family, the late Hajji Azim Khan, ensured that his sons and grandsons remained committed to their Pir. The arrival of the Salafi Tablighi Jamaat in Pak Kaya split the Hajji family, as the grandsons of the oldest son of Azim Khan, the late Hajji Yunus Khan, ascended to a degree of power as active Amirs of the Tablighi Jamaat. They were the first men to introduce Tablighi Jamaat to the village and implement the Tablighi Jamaat's practices, including a ban on watching TV in the households, requiring a half-foot beard for the men, and an end to hosting Pirs by individual families.

The family patriarch, Azim Khan, had four children and the families of two older sons -- the late Hajji Yunus Khan and the late Hajji Daud Khan -- enjoys a close personal relationship because the latter's son is married to the former's daughter. In Pashtun culture, the marital relationship brings people together. Hajji Daud Khan's only son, a lawyer, is married to a daughter of Hajji Yunus Khan. In addition, Hajji Daud Khan's other daughter is married to a son of Hajji Yunus Khan, a pair of marriages that brought the two families even closer together. Hajji Daud Khan's son Shoab Khan, also a lawyer, joined the Tablighi Jamaat and is now an active member of the movement. However, Hajji Yunus Khan's two other brothers continued to be active supporters of the Sufi Pirs. Hajji Yunus Khan's younger brother, Hajji Suliaman Khan, in his call to every prayer (Azan) continued to start the prayer with Zakr, a Sufi practice prohibited by the Tablighi Jamaat. Hajji Yunus Khan's other brother, Hajji Ayub Khan, and his family remains committed to traditional Sufi ideology and practices and the family was noted for hosting the Pir of Ali Sharif and Pir of Jalbai in their guest house. During the late Hajji Ayub Khan's funeral in November 2010, these Pirs practiced some Sufi rituals that infuriated the Salafi Tablighi Jamaat, who viewed these practices as "badaith" (prohibited in Islam) and the Salafi Tablighi Jamaat members almost walked out of the funeral services.

Interestingly, Hajji Suliaman Khan was a committed disciple of the Pirs while his sons were active members of Tablighi Jamaat and tension was created within Hajji Suleiman Khan's family. In contrast, all three sons of Hajji Ayub Khan remain committed to the Pirs.

Another prominent elder of Hajji Family was Hajji Khalil Khan, a strong supporter of the Pir of Jilbai. Khalil was seen hosting the Pir with lavish lunches and dinners and was also observed debating with the Tablighi Jamaat members on the issue of the Sufism vs. Salafism. In contrast, Khalil's sons, all of whom are college graduates and two are medical doctors, were supporters of the Tablighi Jamaat.

It is interesting to note that age and education were the major drivers of this change from traditional Sufi practices to the Salafi Tablighi practices. Illiterate older men continue to follow traditional Sufism while the younger educated generation, which was more cosmopolitan and worked in the modern sector of the economy, followed Tablighi Jamaat and its Salafi ideology. After the deaths of the older, Sufi-oriented generation, the entire tribe's shift toward the Tablighi Jamaat may accelerate dramatically.

A similar fissure is visible within other Jehangir Khel families. For example, the powerful Khabli family was also divided on the issue of whether to follow Sufi practices or shift to the Salafi Tablighi Jamaat. Hajji Man Khan and his brothers were strong followers of Challa Badshah and some other Sufi Pirs while one of the Hajji Man Khan's sons was an Amir of the Tablighi Jamaat. Man Khan's other sons were also active members of the Tablighi Jamaat. Interestingly, Hajji Man Khan's brothers were strong supporters of the Sufis while his sons followed the predictable pattern and became active followers of the Tablighi Jamaat, highlighting the consistently occurring split between the fathers and their male children.

On the issue of Sufism vs. Salafism, the adult children appear to be pitted against their parents and this has provided the mullahs and their immediate family members an opportunity to actively preach the Deobandi Salafi ideology. The village mullahs and their families and the younger generation of tribesmen are connected ideologically with one another on the issue of Tablighi Jamaat and the division between young and the old tribesmen or divisions within families that has been simmering for few years now. Fortunately, this tension has not reached a boiling stage where there is violence as has occurred in both the Khyber Agency and FATA. The Tablighi Jamaat has failed to enforce their practices on each family's members, but the Tablighi leaders and their followers have been gaining more and more support. A delicate balance within the families appears to remain, at least for now. As this balance shifts in favor of either group, and more likely to move toward the Tablighi Jamaat, the latter may begin to use force to impose their practices on the more reluctant other tribesmen.

There are numerous built-in social safety nets that have prevented a violent clash between the two groups. Intermarriages among the families, family cohesiveness, respect for parents and the elderly as required by Pashtunwali, and inter-family alliances on non-religious issues appear to be preventing the tribe from falling apart for now. Both groups have been asserting themselves in the village and it is possible that the two groups could eventually resort to violence in an attempt to silence their opponents. For example, the division between the Sufi and Salafi groups has translated into violence in other parts of the region. In the Khyber Agency, two sectarian groups – the Sufi Ansar-ul Islam and Salafi Tablighi Jamaat Tehrik-e-Islam – have been actively fighting on this religious issue for years.

For now, religious tension simmers peacefully within the families in the village. Numerous social and economic safety nets are holding the families together and preventing any wedge that may lead to a violent confrontation between the two groups in the village. This religious change has been gradual and non-violent so far and the Tablighi Jamaat appears to desire to keep it that way because the Tablighi members are aware that history is on their side. They know that the tribe has been shifting toward Tablighi Jamaat's ideology and they believe it is just a matter of time before the whole tribe adopts its way of thinking.

It is possible that the entire Jehangir Khel tribe one day will switch from Sufism to Salafism. It is also possible that this change will remain evolutionary. Since the Tablighi Jamaat is a Pan-Islamic movement, a shift from Sufism to Salafism may actually enhance tribal unity. The members and the Amirs of the Tablighi Jamaat from other fractured tribes may unite on the Tablighi platform. Tablighi Jamaat members were observed meeting with their peers from the Sufi side of the tribe, serving as well as a source of stability and unity.

Additionally, Tablighi Jamaat members were seen sharing human and financial resources. For example, the Tablighi Jamaat members were observed to pool their resources for renting vehicles for their trip to annual Ijtama (gathering) in Rawind near Lahore. The Amirs were seen mediating disputes among the families. Since the Amirs are perceived as religious, selfless and credible, they are likely to be called upon for more mediation services, services that were provided either by the Pirs or the traditional tribal leaders in the past, further enhancing their influence and raising their profiles in the area.

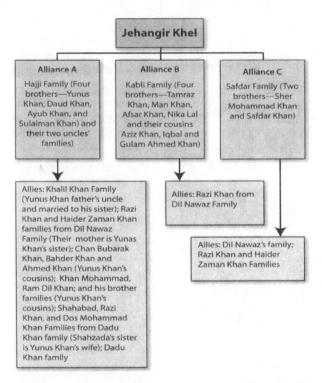

Figure 4. Major Family Alliances within the Jehangir Khel

Comparing Pashtunwali with Tablighi Jamaat

Tablighi Jamaat's influence has been changing the village of Pak Kaya where numerous traditional practices have been halted due to the Tablighi influence, and increasing conservative religiousness in the village. Figure 5 lists the differences between Pashtunwali and Islam.

Pashtunwali	Salafi Islam
Emphasis on revenge, acts that enhances the power and prestige of a person, family.	Stresses forgiveness within the Muslim community while advocating violence toward infidels, acts which tribesmen convinced by militants as more honorable and power and prestige enhancing.
Hospitality and accommodation for outsiders, dependents (hamsaya), or with a tribal elder or a leader, acts that carries prestige and respect.	Preaches accommodation of and respect for Islamic militants while requiring that tribesmen view them as "jihadists" (Islamic warriors), status making them superior to the tribesmen.
Exalts personal, family, or tribal achievement, often generating jealousy within peer groups.	Minimize personal, family, or tribal achievement as "God-given," to avoid individual achievement to reduce potential jealousy.
Focus on personal and tribal identity to achieve individual status; a beneficial process that may also create feuds, fragmentation, and cleavage between jealous individuals.	Highlight Pan-Islamic identity in attempt to create harmony, unity, and a common Muslim identity crossing the tribal boundaries, possibly as an initial phase toward eventual radicalization.
Draws attention to personal, family, tribal empowerment and accomplishments to bring more prestige and influence to enhance power.	Focus on sacrifice by the individual, family, and tribe for a greater Pan-Islamic cause.
Encourage parties in a dispute to pursue peace through a jirga process that provides conflict prevention and conflict resolution, not justice.	Force parties to negotiate to end conflict with an emphasis on punishing the aggressor to achieve justice.

Pashtunwali	Salafi Islam
Require that tribesmen follow and respect the leadership of tribal elders.	Command tribesmen to follow the Amirs' guidance irrespective of the Amir's age.
Sources of power are family and tribal alliances.	Source of power is religious, traditional Islam.
Recognize mullahs as prayer leaders.	Consent to both mullahs and Amirs as prayer leaders.
Tolerate music and folk dancing.	Ban music and dancing.
Tolerate men without beards.	Require tribesmen to grow beards.
Tolerate smoking, use of hashish, opium, and other drugs.	Prohibit smoking and use of other drugs.
Tolerate television and theaters.	Ban television and theaters.

Figure5. Pashtunwali and Salafi Islam – A Comparison.

Specific Changes Observed in Pak Kaya

The use of hashish was accepted: In the past, some people were observed smoking hashish in the hujra, but now no one smokes hashish openly in the village. Previously, there was widespread use of tobacco, especially in a Cheelam (a water pipe, or hookah). The religious leader, Challa Badshah, visited the village, but he would not attend prayers and instead he and his followers would openly smoke hashish. Some of his followers would sing and dance throughout the night. Currently, Challa Badshah has nearly stopped visiting the village and when he visits the area, he either camps outside the village or stays in a less visible private house.

Music and dance were allowed: Traditionally, the young men would hold bachelor parties during a wedding ceremony. The young men would go to a city secretly invite female dancers and, with the exception of a few older religious men, the whole village's male population would watch the female dancers' performance. The village women were not allowed to participate due to gender segregation, but a wedding was a real celebration where young people would bring in musicians, drummers, and female dancers who would perform festivities for two days. Even the village mullah turned a blind eye to these events. All this changed with the entry of the Tablighi Jamaat's influence and since the mid 1990's now no one dares to hold events like this. A marriage ceremony now involves only a lunch feast where music and dancing is not allowed.

Wrestling and kabbadi: Every spring and summer, young men would wrestle to allow the men to show their strength by participating in this form of athletics while the whole village watched the event. Since the mid 1990's, the appearance of the Amirs, this practice has stopped. Kabbadi was another popular game in the village in which the young men would show their strength by participating in various games, but this has also been halted.

Mukha: This was a spring archery competition for young men in which players were divided into two teams and that would compete with each other. After selecting the best team in the tribe, the village would set up a competition with surrounding tribes in a match that would be watched by all the tribesmen. The Tablighi Amirs do not like this practice, but they have not been able to halt it completely. They have successfully reduced interest in the archery contest and there has been less enthusiasm than before when it was a major event.

Volleyball: Volleyball remains very popular among the young villagers. Tablighi Jamaat has not acted against it, allowing the young men to play volley ball every evening. Competition is still held against teams from the surrounding tribes, and this event is watched widely not only by the tribesmen, but also by senior Tablighi Jamaat members.

Dog fighting: Dog fighting has been a long tradition of Pashtuns and the tribesmen used to arrange dogfights in the village. Dog owners from different part of the region would attend what were considered major events. The owners of the dogs would use the events to enhance their influence and prestige among the tribesmen, but now dog fighting has been completely stopped.

Chicken and bird fighting: Rooster fights used to be a major event in the village and the whole tribe would assemble in afternoons to watch the competition. Sometimes, the owners of roosters from surrounding tribes would participate in the fight, which was always a very popular event. Some people would also catch birds, including "Bataras," and hold a fight. Both of these practices have now been stopped.

Gutta: At night after 9 o'clock, the elders would go to their homes to sleep and then the young men who slept in the hujra would play a game with a ring, called "Gutta." The young men would divide into two groups and each would take turns hiding a ring in the closed fists of the participants. The members of the other group would guess who had the ring hidden inside their fist. This used to be a very popular game that allowed the young men to entertain themselves, but this game too has been forbidden since the Tablighi Jamaat and other Salafists view these games as un-Islamic thus have halted them. Tablighi Jamaat's Amirs have even prohibited tribesmen from watching television both in the hujra and in their own homes.

Pashtunwali and Islam

There is a unique relationship between the Pashtun culture and Islam. Most Pashtuns argue that there is no difference between Pashtunwali and Islam and they argue that for a man to be a Pashtun, he must also be a Muslim. This argument may or may not be true, but this study found that Islam has now superseded Pashtunwali when it comes to the Pashtun way of life, or when it comes to decision-making process among Pashtuns. Islamic traditions are now more commonly relied upon than Pashtunwali because Pashtun cultural rules don't provide answers to some of the complex questions raised in the daily lives of the tribesmen as modernization enters their lives. Islam appears to provide solutions to certain problems that Pashtunwali fails to provide. For example, Pashtunwali demands the ancient requirement of an "eye for an eye" when it comes to revenge and this long enduring cycle of revenge can ruin families involved in an active feud. In contrast, Islam stresses forgiveness, which prevents the harmful effect of the cycle of killing required under Pashtunwali's revenge requirement.

Pashtunwali relies upon hereditary leadership while Islam facilitates achieved leadership, which appeals to the young educated tribesmen whose leadership is blocked in traditional Pashtun society. Under Pashtunwali, the age of a person defines influence and power, but in Islam, age does not play an important role in the leadership and piety and religious education and practices are the source of a leadership position.

Pashtunwali lionizes personal, family, and tribal achievement, generating jealousy among close relatives, especially in the male cousins from the paternal side of the family. In contrast, Islam demonizes personal, family, and tribal achievement as "God-given," not individual achievement and this minimizes jealousy and competition among the tribesmen. Pashtunwali glorifies personal and tribal identity that creates feuds and fragmentation within society while Islam highlights a common Islamic identity that facilitates more harmony, unity, and a shared identity that crosses traditional tribal barriers. Pahstunwali draws attention to personal, family, and tribal empowerment that brings more power and prestige to a person, family, or tribe, but in contrast Islam underlines self, family and tribal sacrifice for a higher Islamic cause.

Pashtunwali turns a blind eye toward some un-Islamic practices, including music, dance, smoking, and the use of hashish and opium, while the Islam-based Tablighi Jamaat movement prohibited these practices and views them as un-Islamic.

Under Pashtunwali, a source of power for a man is tribal affiliation and tribal alliances while the source of personal power for a person within Salafism is based exclusively on religion. The leaders under Pashtunwali are elders of the families or Nawabs, Maliks, and Khans. In contrast, the tribesmen accept the Tablighi Amirs as leaders because they are perceived as being selfless, religious, and they demonstrate piety in their daily lives as they set examples to follow.

The traditional Pashtun tribal leadership structure has changed due to modern education, rural-urban migration, trading, an influx of money and remittance from the Middle East, proliferation of media outlets, mobility of the people, and growth of transportation. Modern institutions such as administrative structure, the police force, the court system, and the system of governance, similar to those in the colonial system continue to exist while allowing wide spread corruption and inefficiency.

Pashtun society is layered and the inner most level is the individual, followed by family, then sub-tribe, tribe, and while Islam supersedes everything when it comes to the local decision making process within Pashtun tribal governance. For example, a man's decision may be overruled by the decision of a family; the family's decision can be set aside by a sub-tribe's decision, which in turn may be suspended by the tribe's decision. A tribe's decision can be suspended by decisions made at multiple tribal levels, which in turn is supplanted by any decision believed to be inconsistent with Islamic law. Islam forms the outmost ring of rules applying to governance in Pashtun society. Therefore, in any clash between local cultural dynamics and Islam, the latter prevails.

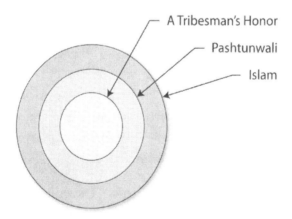

Figure 6. Pashtun Tribal Structure.

Traditionally, Pashtuns followed Sufi Islam and the Pirs who were the guardians of Sufism. The older generation of Pirs were viewed as selfless and were believed to be devoted Muslims extending services and religious advice to the local tribesmen. These Pirs were seen to address some of the issues Pashtunwali failed to correct and while the traditional Pirs were perceived to be religious, neutral and uncorrupt, the new generation of Pirs and their children stopped providing services their ancestors used to provide. Now, the new generations of Pirs are increasingly seen as non-religious, corrupt, and lacking in impartiality when providing guidance and young Pashtuns no longer view the new generation of Pirs as religious and don't view their practices as being based on Islamic values.

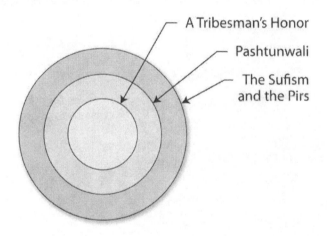

Figure 7. Pashtun Tribal Structure and Sufism Influence.

Since most of the current Pashtuns lack trust in traditional Sufism and the Sufi Pirs as credible representatives of Islam, they search for "pure" Islam and the current generation of tribesmen has found in the piety of the Tablighi Jamaat what they used to see in the earlier generation of Pirs, a selfless devotion to Islam. These Pashtuns view the Tablighi men as religious, pure, selfless, and uncorrupt and it is these characteristics that have been attracting Pashtuns to this new Tablighi reformist movement. The Tablighi Amirs extend mediating services to the local tribesmen and, in addition, the Tablighi Jamaat's Amirs in the village don't abuse their power or use their status to extort money from the tribesmen as the Pirs used to do or the Mullahs have been doing for generations. Amirs provide their services at no cost and expect nothing in return except for the expectation that the tribesmen should practice their version of Islam. The tribesmen respect the Amirs because they view them as honest and religious, the qualities the tribesmen no longer find in the Pirs and the traditional Mullahs.

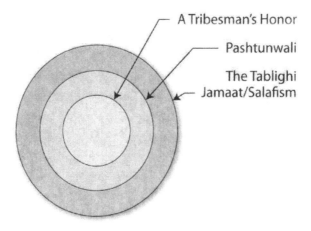

A Tribesman's Honor

Pashtunwali

The Tablighi Jamaat/Salafism

Figure 8. Pashtun Tribal Structure with Sufism Displaced by Salafism.

Salafist Leadership Structure

Within the tribal structure of Pashtun society, super elites who enjoy respect and influence across the tribes in a region, sit at the top of the leadership structure. These super elites compete among themselves to achieve, and then sustain, their leadership positions. Most of these super elites inherited their leadership position while others managed to achieve this position and these super elites make alliances with the sub-elites enjoying the respect and influence over two or more sub-tribes in an area. The super elites' influence depends upon the number of the sub-elites in their "block" or "political alliance" known as "dullahs" in the area. [52]

It was explained in previous studies that a super elite's influence among the Pashtun tribes in the region depends upon how many sub-elites there are within his dullahs or the number of tribal elders in his dullahs. In most of the regions in the Pashtun-inhabited area, the super elites do not have direct access to the elders of the individual families and these super elites depend upon the sub-elites for access or influence on the family elders. The elders have direct influence over the tribesmen and their dependents, and in some instances, a super elite may have a direct beneficial relationship with an influential elder of a family within a sub-tribe.

---

[52] See *Jirgas*: *The Pashtun Way of Conflict Resolution,* by Khan Idris, 2010, http://www.tribalanalysiscenter.com for more detail.

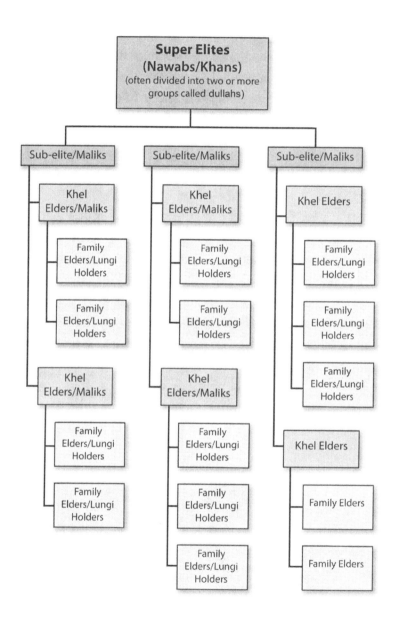

Figure 9. Pashtun Leadership Structure.

Following its general strategy, the Tablighi Jamaat recruited super elites in the area in the 1990s when Faiz Khan, son of Allah Dad Khan, became the first super elite who joined the Tablighi Jamaat to become an Amir. Faiz Khan subsequently recruited a son of Jamil, an influential sub-elite from nearby Anbar village. Faiz Khan's family was one of the richest families in Swabi district and Faiz Khan's father, the late Allah Dad Khan, enjoyed tremendous respect and influence across the tribes in the region. Allah Dad Khan was a Khan, a landlord, from the historical village Hund, but he lived in Anbar, about two miles from Pak Kaya where the Jehangir Khel tribe allied itself with Allah Dad Khan's family. The late Allah Dad Khan was very close to the senior elders of powerful families of Jehangir Khel, including Yunus Khan, the head of the Hajji family, and Tamraz Khan, the leader of the Khabli family. After Allah Dad Khan died, Faiz Khan took the position as the family's super elite.

Faiz Khan, now a Tablighi Jamaat Amir, and Jamil's son, another Tablighi Jamaat Amir, were seen bringing Gasht, a Tablighi Jamaat missionary group to the Jehangir Khel mosque, but Faiz Khan's efforts failed to convert a single tribesman from the Jehangir Khel to the Tablighi movement despite the fact that his family enjoyed tremendous respect and influence in the village. At the time, the tribesmen were observed making fun of the Tablighi Jamaat members when they visited the village.

Faiz Khan was unsuccessful in his attempts to convert the Jehangir Khel tribesmen because the local elders believed so strongly in Sufism. The elders of the major Jehangir Khel families opposed Salafism and continued to strongly support Sufism, and Faiz Khan, as a super elite, did not interact or communicate with the tribesmen directly in his efforts at conversion. It is important to understand that it is difficult, if not impossible, for the super elites to deal directly with the tribesmen due to status consciousness. The elders, and in some instances, the sub-elites, are the individuals interacting with the ordinary tribesmen while the super elites remain above the fray and elders and the sub-elites act as intermediaries between the tribesmen and the powerful super elites.

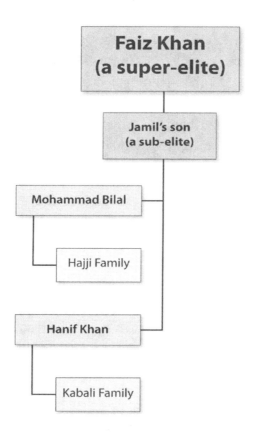

Figure 10. Tablighi Jamaat's in-road into the Jehangir Khel through the Leadership Structure.

While Tablighi Jamaat initially failed to convert the tribesmen because the local Jehangir families remained strong supporters of Sufism, in the late 1990s, two young men from the Jehangir Khel joined Tablighi Jamaat. One, a man named Hanif Khan, converted to Salafism when he was living in the United Kingdom and the other, Bilal, accepted Salafism while he was a graduate student at Peshawar University. Both young men were elevated to senior positions within the Tablighi Jamaat and became Amirs, important positions since Hanif and Bilal were from two powerful Jehangir Khel families: the Kabali and Hajji families, respectively.

With Hanif and Bilal converting, local dynamics changed radically because the Tablighi Jamaat was now able to make serious inroads into the tribe. Both Hanif and Bilal, who were college graduates, converted almost all the young men in the village. The elders of the families who were still Sufis could not use force to stop these young men because they were their sons or grandsons. Hanif was the son of Man Khan, a strong elder from Kabali family and Bilal was a grandson of Yunus Khan, a powerful elder of the Hajji family. Interestingly, the elders remained committed to Sufism as the young men in the village, especially the educated young men, started to join the Tablighi Jamaat. The elders were turning a blind eye to the activities of these Salafi young men rather than attempt to confront members of their own families. In some cases, the young men were becoming "too modern" with use of alcohol and tobacco and the elders may have viewed their newly acquired religious fervor as stabilizing some troubled lives.

Tribal dynamics in the region are likely to shift in favor of the Salafists since they have managed to recruit several important tribal members: Faiz Khan, the super elite, a sub-elite who is the son of Jamil, and the sons of other influential elders of the Jehangir Khel tribe. This could help the Salafists spread their message more effectively at the grassroots level of the village. Tablighi Jamaat only promoted men who were from powerful families to the desirable Amir position and not a single Amir was found to be from dependent families or less influential families. This case study of the Jehangir Khel revealed that the Tablighi Jamaat could make inroads into the tribe only after they converted, and then elevated to the leadership positions, two tribesmen from powerful families. The Tablighi Jamaat's recruitment and then promotion to the leadership position of a super elite and a sub-elite did not help the Salafists influence the local tribesmen. The Jehangir Khel families and the elders of the families resisted the influence of the Salafists, but all of this changed when the Tablighi Jamaat recruited Hanif and Bilal, young men from the targeted age group within Pak Kaya village.

Salafism and Political Alliances

Since it formed in 1924 in India, the Tablighi Jamaat's primary aim has been to start an Islamic spiritual reformation by working at the grass roots level, reaching out to Muslims across all social and economic levels to bring them closer to the historical practices of Prophet Mohammad. Tablighi Jamaat maintains a non-affiliating stature in matters of politics and "fiqh," or Islamic jurisprudence, so as to avoid the controversies that would otherwise accompany such affiliations. Tablighi Jamaat and its members in the village remain apolitical, but this could be temporary since all of the religious maneuvering is occurring in a very dynamic situation.

There are three major political dullahs or political blocs, in the village—the Awami National Party (ANP), Pakistan Peoples' Party (PPP), and Pakistan's Muslim League Nawaz (PML-N)—and each are led by a super elite in the area. In the region, the ANP dullahs was headed by Salim Khan while Iftikhar Khan headed the PML-N dullahs, and Khan of Zaida headed the PPP dullahs.

The super elites and the local elders either interact through sub-elites or directly with their supporters in the village. For example, Salim Khan is an ANP leader in Swabi district and his influence over the Jehangir Khel's families is not direct, but through a sub-elite, Khurshad Bacha from Kunda village who has direct influence over Safdar, Saddique, and Jam Dad's family.

In contrast, the PPP regional super elite, the Khan of Zaida, has a direct relationship with Shamsee from Tur Deri village. Both Khan and Shamsee enjoy good relationships with Tamraz Khan, an elder of Khabali family, and the Dil Nawaz and Shoab Khan Families directly support Shamsee and Khan, the local PPP leaders. It is worth noting that Shoab Khan, a lawyer, is from the Hajji family, but Shoab Khan's mother is from the Khabali family and Shoab Khan, instead of supporting his paternal uncles, supports his maternal uncle. In Pashtun society the maternal relationship is stronger than the paternal relationship.

The third block from the PML in the village is headed by Iftikhar Khan, a son of Haji Mustan Khan, a prominent leader of the Muslim League in the area. Due to direct family relationships between the Hajji family and Iftikhar Khan's family, the Hajji family decided to join the PML, along with

Dost Mohammad's and Dadu Khan's families. These families supported Iftikhar Khan in the 2008 election.

The Hajji family continues to enjoy a good relationship with ANP bloc headed by Khurshad Bacha and Salim Khan. It is worth noting that Dost Mohammad's and Dadu Khan's families always side with the Hajji family because Dost Mohammad's sister is married to Yunus Khan and Dadu Khan's wife is a sister of Bader Khan, who is also a member of the Hajji family.

These dullahs alliances were relatively stable. The Jehangir Khel families remained loyal to the respective political groups for a number of years. For example, Tamraz Khan and his Kabli family had been supporters of PPP since the 1970s. Except for the Kabali family, the Jehangir Khel supported the ANP in past elections. However, the Hajji family joined with Iftikhar Khan, a PML super elite in the 2002 election because Khan enjoys a personal relationship with some members of the Hajji family. When the Hajji family switched their loyalty from ANP to PML, Dadu Khan's and Dost Mohammad's families, allies of the Hajji family, also joined PML while Safdar Khan's family continued to support the ANP. Currently, the Jehangir Khel is divided into three major political groups with the Mullah's family continuing to support a religious political party, Jamiat-u-Islam Fazul (JUI-F). Predictabily, the Mullah's family was the only family in the village that supported JUI-F since he was also associated with the Deobandi Movement.

The Jehangir Khel's gradual descent to Salafism has not impacted the political grouping yet since the Tablighi Jamaat continues to enjoy support from across all the political groups. And this has given the Salafists an opportunity to stay above the political divisions within the village and the tensions that come from the rowdy politics in Pakistan while the apolitical status of the Tablighi Jamaat further enhanced the influence of the Amirs, who are perceived as politically neutral.

Salafism appears to create an apolitical affinity among its members and the Tablighi Jamaat's Amirs were not observed to vote in the 2008 election nor did they endorse any candidate. The Tablighi Jamaat's main emphasis continued to focus on proselytizing the villagers as the Tablighis focus their efforts in teaching against Sufism and Sufi practices, and they were not observed to be making any public political statements. The members of the Tablighi Jamaat now come from almost all the families of the tribe.

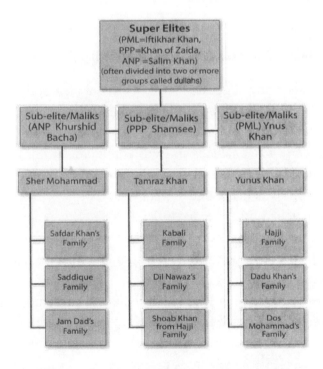

Figure 11. Political Blocs within the Jehan Khel Tribe.

The Tablighi Jamaat appears to have made broad political inroads into the entire Jehangir Khel tribe. Key Tablighi Jamaat Amirs, Hanif and Bilal, came from PML and PPP and almost all the young men from the Khabli and Hajji Families joined the Tablighi Jamaat and this religious connection seems to be more powerful than their political and family affiliations. Their Salafi affiliation appears to be much stronger than any of their political and tribal affiliation and unlike Sufism, which did not interfere with a tribesman's participation in a political action group, Salafism appears to interfere within political affiliations. Tablighi Jamaat members seem to distance themselves from active politics and their Jamaat's neutrality appears to be helping its members reach out to everyone in the tribe.

The Tablighi Jamaat: A Source of Stability

This study suggests that in its initial stages, at least, the Tablighi Jamaat may be bringing stability to the local tribal structure. As the traditional tribal society gives way to the forces of modernity that includes modern communications, electronic media, access to cities and roads, modern education and a greatly improved economic system, the Tablighi Jamaat and its Islamic practice brings order to local society. It is important to understand that the modern governing institutions, such as the police, justice, and political administration either do not exist in a modern sense in Pakistan's villages or have failed to keep up with the ever-changing local environment. The traditional tribal structure, which has been keeping the local fractured sub-tribes together, has been under tremendous pressure due to rapid changes caused by the forces of change and in the absence of modern governance, the local tribesmen are turning to the

Tablighi Jamaat and Salafi practices that appear to bring stability and order to rural society. The tribesmen who used to turn to local Pirs and their Sufi practices during turbulent periods or when Pashtunwali's traditional rules of behavior failed to resolve local issues are now turning to the Tablighi Jamaat because villagers now view Pirs and Sufism as un-Islamic, corrupt, and lacking credibility.

The new generations of Pashtuns living along the Afghan-Pakistan border no longer view Sufism as a credible alternative to Pashtunwali and the young tribesmen think that the Pirs and the Sufis exploit the tribes for personal gain. They are dropping traditional Sufi practices and turning to the Tablighi Jamaat and Salafi practices because they have found some positive elements in Salafi practices that they no longer see in Sufism. The tribesmen also find the traditional culture of Pashtunwali to be useless in the rapidly changing environment where the Tablighi Jamaat Amirs appear to bring stability and prevent and resolve conflict.

Case Study: Hajji Man Khan and Hajji Yunus Khan bought some land together near the village and during the demarcation of the land; a dispute broke out between the two tribal elders. Both elders were from two powerful families of the Jehangir Khel – the Hajji and Khabli families. The incident had the potential to drag the whole village into open conflict as each elder was expected to get support from not only from his own extended family but also from allies in other families. Master Mohammad Zaman, an Aso Khel elder from Bar Kaya village, and Mulvi Omar from the Mullah family were the first ones to sense the impending danger. Both elders initiated the mediation process by secretly meeting members of both families in attempts to resolve their differences. Both Master Mohammad Zaman and Mulvi Omar enjoyed an excellent relationship with the Hajji and Khabli families and both elders were perceived as being neutral in the dispute, a critical element which helped the elders play their mediating role.

Both Zaman and Omar visited the area and measured the land prior to delivering a final decision to both Yunus Khan and Man Khan. Man Khan agreed to the settlement, but he claimed that a path on the side of the road also belonged to him. He also claimed that this path gave about 2/8 of an acre more land to Yunus Khan's family. Yunus Khan was furious over Man Khan's claim. In order to provoke Yunus Khan, Man Khan dumped some dirt on a service road which raised the level of the road, blocking the natural water flow from Yunus Khan's land to Man Khan's land and onward to the nearby Indus River. In retaliation for Man Khan's action, Yunus Khan told the peasant sharecroppers on his land to plant trees on two acres of the land that was contiguous to Man Khan's land. Yunus Khan's action was a punitive measure to take revenge against Man Khan, and the trees planted negatively impacted the productivity of Man Khan's land.

The tension between the two men increased daily and there was a good chance that both men would be engaged in open conflict, dragging the Hajji and the Khabli families into the fight. A conflict between these two powerful families would certainly engulf the whole tribe and in late November 2009, Man Khan visited his land where he exchanged some harsh words with Yunus Khan's peasants over some bushes on the side of the service road. Man Khan was furious, but the peasants outnumbered him so he did not take any direct action. Man Khan returned to the village and complained to the sons of Yunus Khan about the incident where Yunus Khan's sons assured Man Khan they would investigate the matter and take action against their peasants.

Yunus Khan's sons told their peasants to drop the matter because they did not want to aggravate the tension between the two families. Man Khan sent his sons to the area to provoke the peasants who did not challenge Man Khan's sons. The situation was explosive because Man Khan thought Yunus Khan was using his peasants as a proxy to humiliate him, a claim denied by the Hajji family, while Yunus Khan neither accepted nor denied Man Khan's claim and was quite pleased that Man Khan was humiliated.

Man Khan met with one of the sons of Yunus Khan and formally protested the incident. One of Yunus Khan's sons assured him that his father had not been involved as he also explained to Man Khan that he would not do anything to "dishonor any Jehangir Khel tribesman, let alone his own uncle, Man Khan." This assurance and respect shown to Man Khan helped defuse the situation, but Man Khan's sons were equally furious and were ready to initiate a conflict with the peasants, who enjoyed the protection of the Hajji family, in order to reclaim the honor of their father. Any attack against the peasants would have seen by the Hajji family as a provocation, likely triggering open conflict between the two families. In Pashtun culture, a landowner is responsible for the protection of his peasants and in addition, is also responsible for the behavior of his peasants. If a landowner believes that a peasant is a troublemaker, he evicts the peasant and his family from his land. In this situation, Yunus Khan's sons assured Man Khan and his family that they would investigate the matter regarding the behavior of their peasants. It would have been dishonorable for the Hajji family if Man Khan's sons attacked the peasants, especially after Yunus Khan's sons became involved and assured Man Khan that they would investigate the incident and punish the peasants if they were at fault.

In Pashtun society, either honor or an attack on honor can fuel a conflict. An incident involving honor and the reputation of a family and how the incident is managed may have a huge impact on future events. There are numerous built-in mechanisms within Pashtunwali that prevent a small incident like this from turning into a major issue. Small incidents can result in conflict between two individuals, which can certainly plunge their respective families into conflict and once fighting begins between two individuals, their respective families automatically support their tribe's side and once conflict begins honor requires individuals to side with one's own family member. If a physical fight breaks out between two tribesmen from different tribes, preservation of honor requires every tribesman to support his tribe. Once blood is spilled, any tribesman who does not join the fight is dishonored, and is perceived to be a coward.

In this case, both Man Khan and Yunus Khan were parties to the conflict and it was more honorable for Yunus Khan's sons to side with the peasants, and it was equally honorable for Yunus Khan to side with Man Khan, his tribesman, because this fight was between their uncle and the peasants. If the situation spun out of control and degenerated into a fight between the peasants and Man Khan, Yunus Khan's sons would have either mediated between the two parties or they would have expelled the peasants from their land. Incidents like these happen often in Pashtun society, and local elders quickly intervene to resolve them before open fighting starts.

As explained previously, there are two senior Tablighi Amirs from these two powerful families of Man Khan and Yunus Khan. Sensing the approaching danger, both Amirs met and then told their elders to desist in their efforts to mediate the matter. They told the elders that they would resolve this matter according to the tenets of Islam and in Pashtun society, Islam supersedes Pashtunwali.

In this situation, Man Khan's honor was compromised because the low class peasants exchanged harsh words with him. Pashtun culture required that Man Khan reclaimed his honor by punishing the peasants and Man Khan was justified in asking his extended family to punish the peasants. Pashtunwali also required that the Hajji Family sided with Man Khan on this matter because the men from the dependent peasants' families "dared to exchange harsh words with Man Khan," an exchange perceived as dishonorable act against Man Khan.

In Pashtun society peasants and young men are expected to respect elders. Any slight in this matter is viewed as a violation of Pashtunwali, so it is therefore viewed as honorable for the Hajji family to support their peasants, especially if they were not at fault since Man Khan provoked the incident. However, the Hajji family did not support their peasants openly because Pashtunwali required that the Hajji family support their own tribesman against any outsider. In addition, the Pashtunwali requirement superseded the personal requirement of honor, forcing the Hajji family to tell the peasants to stand down on the matter.

When the pair of Tablighi Amirs intervened and asked everyone to cease their arguments, everyone listened to them once they stated that they would decide the matter according to the tenets of Islam. Neither of the Tablighi Amirs had any religious education. The Amir from the Hajji Family, Bilal, was a computer professor at a university and the Amir from the Khabli family, Hanif, was a college graduate running his family business. Neither of them had any formal religious education, but they were well respected as religious men by the villagers involved in the dangerous incident.

Both Tablighi Amirs held a series of jirgas to collect facts and finally announced their decision on the matter that both families accepted but with Man Khan grumbling about the results, but he could not challenge the decision of the Amirs because one of the Amirs was his own son. The Amirs blamed Man Khan for provoking the peasants, but they also ordered the peasants not to respond to Man Khan in the future even if he provoked them.

Salafism and Tribal Fissures

Changes within any traditional society have never been orderly, but Salafism's penetration into generally conservative Pashtun communities has been pretty revolutionary up to now. It appears that the Tablighi Jamaat's strategy is working as they have been peacefully preaching their message, that jihad is within each individual. Despite some resistance from the supporters of Sufism and periodic provocations from the supporters of the Pirs, Tablighi Jamaat members have remained peaceful in the village since they first appeared. In addition, the

Tablighi Jamaat's members have not viewed any arguments against their positions nor have any of them been challenged by the Sufis as a matter of honor. The Tablighi Jamaat members appear to believe that history and time are on their side and that the Pirs and their ideology are exploitative of the tribesmen. As the tribes gradually become more modern and educated, the Tablighi believe the tribesmen will drop their support for the Pirs and their traditional practices in favor of Tablighi Jamaat.

Tablighi Jamaat's method of infiltration into the tribes appears to involve the recruitment of members of powerful families. They appear to know that to make inroads into traditional Pashtun society, they must proselytize with the more credible and powerful voice in the communities and they have been successful with this strategy.

Case Study: Tablighi Jamaat's first recruit in the area was son of Allah Dad Khan, the largest landowner in the Swabi district. Allah Dad Khan's son, Faiz Khan, was the first person who joined Tablighi Jamaat in the 1990s and he was the first of the super elite families in the area to join the new movement. Soon, Faiz Khan became a prominent Amir of the Tablighi Jamaat and recruited the son of another prominent family member living in Anbar village, located about two miles from Pak Kaya. These people were known locally as "Jamil's family" and this was one of most powerful families in the area. Both of the newly minted Amirs were soon preaching Islam and would also visit Pak Kaya as missionaries for the new strand of Islam. However, despite the efforts of these two Amirs, the Tablighi Jamaat failed to make any inroads into the Jehangir Khel because most of the prominent families of the tribe continued to support Sufism.

All of this changed when Hanif, Man Khan's son from the Khabli family, returned from the United Kingdom where he had been recruited into the Tablighi Jamaat. The Tablighi Jamaat also converted Bilal, a computer professor in a university, when he was a student at Peshawar University. When these two tribesmen from prominent families entered Tablighi Jamaat, local village dynamics changed dramatically. Both of the new Amirs advocated Tablighi Jamaat and its practices and were quickly promoted to the highest rank within the movement. They soon converted nearly all of the young tribesmen in the village and also started challenging the elders who still followed traditional Sufism.

Soon, the Tablighi Jamaat was enmeshed in almost every family in the Jehangir Khel tribe. Traditionally, the families which make up a sub-tribe in Pashtun society would make a united stand on any issue, but the Tablighi Jamaat's penetrations into these families has been dividing them from within. This multiple series of splits is between the younger generation and the older generations as well as between educated and uneducated tribesmen. For example, Hanif Khan's father and his uncles remained strong supporters of Pirs while Mohammad Bilal's grand uncles and cousins remain strong supporters of Sufism and the Pirs, but with almost all the Tablighi Jamaat members being college graduates, the separation is across both educational and age lines and creates tension within the families.

Case Study: Hajji Ayub Khan died in late November 2010 and belonged to the powerful Hajji family. Ayub Khan and his sons remained strong supporters of the Pirs and Sufism. During the funeral, Ayub Khan's family invited some Pirs who took turns in the ceremony by practicing Zakir, which, as noted previously, the Salafi condemn. The Salafists prefer to have funerals without speeches or rituals and want only a funeral prayer. After the prayer, they insist on burying bodies quickly while Sufi Pirs like to recite Zakir before the actual burial. In this funeral, when the Pirs started Zakir, a larger number of the Salafist supporters protested since they viewed the practice as un-Islamic. Undaunted, the Pirs completed their rituals and finished the ceremony with the prayer and the actual burial while some locals who followed Salafism threatened to boycott the funeral.

Some Sufi Islam followers have continued to follow traditional rituals. For example, Sufis were observed reciting Zakir and praising the Prophet before and after every Azan (the call for prayer) while the Tablighi Jamaat members were observed mocking this practice as they also called it a "Salato" (Salat means prayer). It is interesting that the Mullah did not approve of their use of Zakir in the funeral ceremony, but he still tolerated it. In the past, a few Sufi followers recited Zakir at night on the mosque loudspeaker to disturb the peace while intentionally provoking the Salafis. These Sufism followers recited Zakir in an apparent attempt to convey to the Tablighi Jamaat Salafists in the village that they remained in charge of the mosque.

Salafism and Traditional Pashtun Leadership

The Pashtun tribes inhabiting both sides of the Pakistan-Afghanistan border gradually have been gravitating toward Salafism since the 1990s. In the past, the Sufi Pirs and Sufism, in general, would co-exist with the traditional leadership structure and instead of challenging the tribal leadership, the Pirs and the followers of Sufism would assist in perpetuating the traditional tribal leadership by supporting it. The Pirs, local Khans, and the maliks have coexisted for centuries and sometimes the traditional leaders would use the Pirs and their blessings to ensure the continuity of their power within local communities, while the Pirs and traditional leaders worked to prevent any attempt by firebrand mullahs to take control over local tribes. In the instances where mullahs did manage to take control, the Pirs and local leaders quickly wrested power back away from the mullahs.

Modern Wahhabi-based Salafism and the guardians of this form of Salafism are different than the revolutionary mullahs of the past and are best viewed as being divided into two groups among the Pashtuns. One group is known as active Taliban who only claim to be Tablighi Jamaat members and do not follow the true spirit of Tablighi Jamaat since they use force and violence to enforce principles of Salafism. In contrast, actual Tablighi Movement members don't rely upon violence to enforce the rules of Salafism. Both groups follow the same Salafi ideology and both have been undermining the traditional axis of the Pirs and the Pashtun leaders, but the Taliban and their supporters in Al-Qa'ida have even resorted to killing the local Pirs and traditional leaders in order to gain and maintain control. If the reports are correct, over 200 senior tribal leaders have been killed in last decade in the South Waziristan alone. The Salafists have also been destroying Sufi shrines, a major source of the Pirs' financial and social power and Pakistan's Taliban went as far as bombing the shrine of a special Sufi Pir, Rehman Baba, near Peshawar in 2010. In many ways, the violence seen in Pakistan's border regions with Afghanistan may be defined in terms of a conflict between traditional Sufism and the imported new interpretation of Islam, Salafism.

While it is not worrisome that Pashtun tribesmen are turning toward this new brand of Islam while becoming more religious, a major concern involves the fact that the tribesmen are using this form of Salafism to challenge state control in both Pakistan and Afghanistan. Additionally, Pashtun Salafists use Salafism as a justification to invite Al-Qa'ida members and other political activists into their organizations. Once empowered with both this new ideology along with new human and material resources, Pashtuns quickly rebel against the traditional tribal and religious leadership and use their newly gained power to destroy the existing tribal and religious structures in order to ensure their own primacy continues. Once the existing tribal and religious structures are destroyed, chaos results to create situations that could quickly be filled by far more radical elements such as the Taliban and Al-Qa'ida.

Interestingly, the leaders of this form of radical Salafism have worked to undermine not only the traditional tribal leadership and the Sufi Pirs, but also seek to replace the traditional Deobandi mullahs who have tried to coexist peacefully with both the Pirs and the tribal leaders. For example, the Taliban killed Maulana Hasan Jan, was a well-known Deobandi cleric in Peshawar and an acknowledged member of Tablighi Jamaat. He was killed by the Taliban because he issued a Fatwa stating clearly that suicide was forbidden in Islam. In addition to this murder, in March and April 2011, the Taliban tried to kill the leader of Jamiat-ul-Islam, Fazul Rehman, a well-known Pashtun Deobandi cleric who is politically active in Pakistan.

In contrast to the violent Tehrik-i Taliban and Al-Qa'ida tactics, the members of the Tablighi Jamaat have been very peaceful and have even been resolving feuds in Pak Kaya village. As noted earlier, when the Hajji and Khabli families were involved in a land dispute, the Tablighi Amirs intervened and resolved the matter. As previously explained, these Tablighi Jamaat Amirs lack formal religious education and they are also young, but in spite of these limitations, the Amirs took over the decision-making process in some areas and dictated their decisions while using Islam as the justification for their actions and decisions.

It is not only religion that empowers these Tablighi Amirs, but also their tribal linage that enhances their personal standing. Most of these Amirs come from powerful families, and mix their tribal capital with religious capital, making them very powerful in local society. The Pirs and the traditional Mullahs did not enjoy absolute power because they had only religious capital and lacked the necessary tribal status. For tribal capital, the Pirs and traditional mullahs had to depend upon an alliance with local traditional tribal leaders.

In Pashtun society, there is always a balance of power between the religious forces and tribal forces, but this balance could be disturbed if there was an external threat to Islam. At that point, the mullahs would attempt to mobilize the local tribes against the external enemy. Once the mullah, who had religious capital, would grab control of the tribe, there was war and violence. The traditional leaders would get sidelined to allow the mullah to lead the tribe during warfare. The mullahs would stir up excitement among the tribesmen and wage the conflict. Traditionally, mullahs were always supported by the young tribesmen, who joined the mullahs to prove their warfare and leadership skills.

As time passed in these situations, tribal capital has gravitated back to the traditional Pashtun leaders as the balance between the religious and tribal forces returned to equilibrium. This division of power created checks and balances within the Pashtun community and traditional leaders jealously protected their power and influence. They also maintained a check on both the Pirs and the mullahs to ensure that neither could encroach upon the power and influence of traditional Pashtun leaders. Due to the low status of the clerical class, traditional Pashtun leaders do not educate their children to be mullahs, a profession that is looked down upon by the local tribesmen.

The Tablighi Jamaat and Salafism phenomenon are completely different than anything that has been experienced previously in Pashtun society because the Amirs have managed to accrue both religious and tribal authority. Once they acquired religious status, they mixed this with traditional tribal power to become extremely powerful and as a result, the Amirs not only challenge the tribal leaders, but also challenge the local religious leadership within both the Deobandi and Sufi communities. Some Deobandi mullahs quickly sided with the Tablighi Jamaat Amirs in order to gain some protection from being attacked both physically and religiously by their followers and advocates.

Within the village, both Bilal and Hanif became very powerful Amirs because they possessed both the religious and tribal power and they were from powerful families of the Jehangir Khel tribe. As a result, both men were able not only to challenge the traditional tribal leaders in the Jehangir Khel but also the mullahs in the village.

As long as these Amirs remain peaceful, the presence of the Tablighi Jamaat and its Salafist ideology will be a positive force in the community. Their presence has prevented violence and eliminated the use of drugs while they also play a significant role in the local mediation process. However, if these Amirs choose force to enforce their brand of Salafism, there is likely to be violence between them and the residual Sufi advocates in Pak Kaya. While the role of the Amirs and the Tablighi Jamaat in the village was observed to be very peaceful and positive, the Amirs in some other areas in the FATA and Swat opted to use violence to enforce Salafism doctrines and the results have been disastrous. For example, Gul Bahadur is an Amir in North Waziristan who enjoys both religious and the tribal control and this mix of religious and tribal power, along with a willingness to turn to violence, has made him one of the most powerful Amirs in the region.

Agenda of the Tribal Salafists

As noted previously, local Salafists affiliated with Tablighi Jamaat are unique because they not only threaten the traditional tribal structure, but they also endanger the local religious structure, both traditional Sufism and Deobandism. Two questions related to their motivation quickly emerge: What do the Tablighi Jamaat Amirs want and how are they structured? Answers to these questions are complicated because there are a wide variety of Salafi groups operating in the Pashtun-inhabited areas and while the Tablighi Jamaat remains peaceful and its stated objectives remain the basically preaching of Islam as a renewal of faith, there are different groups who claim to be affiliated with Tablighi Jamaat whose activities are not in line with Tablighi Jamaat's philosophy and activities.

Basically, the Tablighi Jamaat Amirs want to transform the tribal way of life since they believe that there are evils all around the Pashtun areas and that Pashtun culture has been corrupted. From their point of view, the traditional leaders and their ancient beliefs, such as Sufism, are part of the problem. The Amirs further believe that traditional tribal and religious leaders contribute to the social, political, and economic ills faced by the Pashtun people and the only way to cure all of these ills in Pashtun society requires the purification of the local society. The way to purify the local society involves the religious renewal of the local tribesmen.

These Amirs believe that if the local tribesmen join the Tablighi Jamaat and follow the practices of Salafi Islam, they would be at peace with themselves and with the surrounding tribes. They want the tribesmen to stop indulging in activities which they believe are un-Islamic, including smoking hashish, using drugs, listening to music, dancing, and watching television. They believe that if the tribesmen stop indulging in these activities they would become pure Muslims and once everyone is pure, local society would be pure, free of violence, drugs, and other ills.

It is difficult to determine what the long-term political goals of the Tablighi Jamaat might be. Currently, members of Tablighi Jamaat remain neutral in local politics while they dictate their version of Islam to the population. They don't want debates and they don't even entertain the idea of debates about their core ideology. They do not consider that they might be wrong on some issues and in places where they have an

119

opportunity to spread their views, they do it through force. For example, in the village they stopped the locals from watching television and the tribesmen are prohibited from having any entertainment in marriage ceremonies. They also started encroaching on the roles formerly played by the traditional leaders and have replaced these leaders in resolving local disputes. This further raises their profile among the tribesmen and undermines the influence of the traditional leaders.

Tablighi Jamaat's members were also observed to be extremely patient with the local tribesmen. Initially, when the Tablighi Jamaat movement was weak in the village, the Jamaat members would visit and stay in the mosque where they cooked food for themselves. In addition, they were observed to announce after the evening prayer that Tablighi Jamaat members were at the mosque and that this group would preach Islam. Appeals were made for the tribesmen to attend and the Tablighi Jamaat members were observed visiting hujras to ask the men to come to the mosque. Most locals did not respond to their appeal and the Jamaat missionaries would spend three days at the mosque before leaving the village.

By 2010, the Tablighi Jamaat was observed to draw larger crowds to the mosque and they were relatively more aggressive in asking people to come to the mosque. It appears that as the Tablighi Jamaat gained power and influence, they started becoming more forceful with their tactics. In the beginning, Tablighi Jamaat members used persuasion as a method, but as their influence and power grew within the community, they began to use both persuasion and coercion.

In numerous places in the FATA and Khyber Pakhtunkhwa (KP), the local Amirs resort to force to impose the practices of Salafism. For example, Mangal Bagh in Khyber Agency forced people to grow beards and to pray five times daily. In addition, girls are prohibited from going to school where Tablighi Jamaat was able to gain control.

Tablighi Jamaat's influence among the poor classes including the peasant families, the barber's family, the blacksmith, and other dependent families was very weak. Almost all the members of the Tablighi Jamaat were observed to be young, educated men from the main Jehangir Khel families. At the local tribal level, this form of Salafism has not been like liberation theology, as the Salafists attract the younger people from mainly the upper and middle classes.

The open question is why the Tablighi Jamaat has been gaining ground among the Pashtuns. It appears that Tablighi Jamaat's organizational structure and leadership fits well with the Pashtun tribal structure, especially in situations in which the Pashtun tribes are fractured and power and influence has become decentralized. Pashtun leadership structure is layered and at the inner most rings there is a family elder, then clan elders, then sub-elites, and then the super elites, while the Tablighi Jamaat approach appears to adapt to the traditional structure of the Pashtun society. The Tablighi Jamaat's organizational structure is much diffused. Like Pashtun tribes, there are jamaats (parties) at each level. There can be as many jamaats as there are Amirs and there is no limit on the number of Amirs in an area. As within Pashtun society, the status of Amir is an achieved status. This flexibility to accommodate as many Amirs as possible prevents jealousy between the local families and also helps Tablighi Jamaat to develop as many credible voices as possible.

Tablighi Jamaat's recruitment of the Amirs from prominent families helps influence a clan at the local level while recruitment of leaders from key tribal families helps Tablighi Jamaat to spread their message more effectively. Tablighi Jamaat's emphasis on team and collegial work is consistent with tribal society where jirga decisions are also made through consensus.

Tablighi Jamaat's emphasis on the non-controversial issues in an early stage of their preaching has been working very well. This approach gives the Tablighi Jamaat members an opportunity to develop their bona fides as religious, selfless holy men, characteristics that are appealing to local tribesmen because they use the Tablighi Jamaat's members to settle internal conflicts. In the absence of a viable court system, internal conflicts are the main source of potential violence at the local level.

The Tablighi Jamaat does not have a centralized leadership structure and this is consistent with Pashtun tribal leadership that is also decentralized. In addition, the Tablighi Jamaat's recruitment requirements ensure that only rich and credible people make it to leadership positions. For example, one person acquired Amir Status in the Tablighi Jamaat after he spent eight months with the Jamaat. In addition, an Amir has to spend one month annually with the Tablighi Jamaat in order to stay in the Amir position. Numerous short visits are also expected on the weekends. These requirements can only be fulfilled by those who are rich enough to devote the time necessary to fulfill the requirements. Some government officers were seen devoting the required time, and eventually acquired Amir status because the government of Pakistan allowed paid time off for the Tablighi Jamaat's activities. While this is not legal, the government's local managers were afraid to prevent the Tablighi Amirs from going on the required sessions with the Tablighi leadership.

Tablighi Jamaat also appeals to some Pashtun tribesmen because the members have a distinct style of dress, beard, and cap. In addition, Tablighi Jamaat embodies certain characteristics which are consistent with Pashtunwali.

1. It replaces the traditional Pashtun dress, which is a loose trouser and long shirt. It creates a sense of identity among members.
2. It creates unity and solidarity within the membership.
3. Tablighi Jamaat's members are brought together in a common cause.
4. It draws the public's attention.
5. Over a period of time, members enjoy widespread respect among the people, including policemen and other security personnel.
6. Tablighi Jamaat's members are perceived as religious, pious, selfless, and holy. This credibility is maintained with each member by regular prayers five times daily, good behavior in public, absence of drug use and smoking, a high degree of cleanliness, and a non-violent behavior.

The Pashtuns are drawn to these men because these individual characteristics are consistent with being an ideal Pashtun (see Appendix A).

Consequences of the Pashtun Tribal Gravitation to Salafism

The Pashtun shifting toward Salafism has been undermining the traditional tribal, social, and religious structure and this new reformation movement has been changing the tribesmen's life style. The process could continue to undermine the local tribal structure, with the potential to erode, and perhaps even destroy, the traditional tribal and religious leadership found among the Pashtuns. In the absence of any other alternative, including modern governing institutions such as security services and an honest judicial system, the Salafists are likely to fill the vacuum they did in some Pashtun-inhabited parts of Afghanistan.

In Pak Kaya village, there has been a steady introduction of Salafi practices. As noted earlier, Tablighi Jamaat and its members are more visible in the village than they used to be. An annual Ijtama (gathering) of the Tablighi Jamaat draws more members of the tribe than in the past and in November 2003, Tablighi Jamaat leaders in the village rented a bus with 20 seats for the tribesmen, scheduled to leave after sunset for the Tablighi Ijtama in Lahore. By sunset, there were only a small number of young men seen on the bus. The Tablighi Jamaat members offered a free ride to Lahore, free lodging, and food, but despite this generous offer, they could not find enough men to go with them. In November 2010, these same Tablighi Jamaat members rented three buses and by sunset, the buses were packed with men. This time, however, the bus ride, lodging, and food were not free, but every participant was observed contributing money.

In 1990s, there were few young men ever seen with beards in the village, but by 2010 the village had totally changed and hardly any young man was seen without a beard.

There appears to be more religiousness and religiosity in the village than previously observed. This trend could continue to the point at which most of the tribesmen gravitate to religiousness. In the 1980s and 1990s, some of the tribesmen were observed not responding to the call for prayer and they preferred to hang out in the hujras when there was a call for prayer. Some young men would hardly pray at all. By 2010, the tribesmen's general behavior changed, more religiousness was observed, and no men were seen in the hujra during prayer time. Every male in the village, from small boys to old men, was observed to be in the mosque during prayers. During Friday prayers, when the peasants from the nearby settlements joined the villagers to pray, the mosque would fill quickly and there was hardly any open space left in the mosque.

There are some positive consequences of this Salafi influence and increasing religiousness among the tribesmen. There was less use of drugs, heroin, opium, and hashish in the village where in the past, there was widespread use of hashish, but by 2009, none of the tribesmen were observed smoking this drug. In the 1980s and 1990s, there were numerous men from prominent Jehangir Khel families who would smoke hashish and were called "Charsee" and they would gather in the hujra to smoke hashish openly. During a visit by Pir Challa Badshah, the whole hujra was converted into a big party where the men, including the Pir, would smoke hashish the whole night. They would get high (called "Ton") and then begin to dance. The village Mullah, a Deobandi who was against this practice, would turn a blind eye to the event, as did the elders, but by 2010 the use of hashish was no longer observed.

In the past, there were also some heroin addicts in the village. A famous heroin case was the case of Shah Mahar Ustad who was the younger brother of Mullah Omar, a prominent Mullah in a nearby village and a cousin of Mullah Mustafa, the Mullah of the Jehangir Khel. Shah Mahar Ustad, along with some men from a nearby village, would smoke heroin openly, but after Shah Mahar died, there was not a known addict in the village. However, there were known opium users called "opiumees," a derogatory word among the locals.

The use of tobacco and cigarettes has gone down due to the preaching of the Tablighi Jamaat. Traditionally, almost every tribesman would smoke the "Hubble Bubble'" known as the "Chelum" in the village. During the 1980s and 1990s, even young boys were smoking the Chalum. Most men would also smoke the Chelum while women would not smoke at all. By 2010, the use of Chelum had decreased and the presence of the Chelum was less noticeable in public places. There were only four or five men who were observed to smoke the Chelum and they were middle aged. There was not a single young man seen smoking the Chelum.

Cigarette use in the 1980s and 1990s was very limited because it was cheaper to smoke the Chelum and only a small number of people were seen smoking cigarettes. By 2010, only a few people who used to smoke the Chelum were seen smoking cigarettes.

The Tablighi Jamaat movement and its activities have also had a positive impact on the health of the local people. In the past, the tribesmen would go to the Pirs when were faced with any health issue. These Pirs would either pray or provide amulets to the sick person. The tribesmen would also go to

126

medicine men, known locally as "Hakims," who would give homeopathic medicine to the tribesmen. The quality of this medicine was not very good. If a tribesman was bitten by a dog and was taken to Jalbai-Jalsai Pir, he would pray for the man and everyone believed that he would be cured. By 2010, limited numbers of tribesmen were going to the Pir in Jalbai-Jalsai for his healing prayers and instead, the most of tribesmen bitten by a dog would go to the hospital to get injections to prevent rabies. Covering all their bases, some tribesmen would take the rabies injections and also pay a visit to the Pir. In the past all Infant deliveries were handled by a basic midwife, who was illiterate and known as "Dai." Sometimes, due to complications, the infants and their mothers were lost during labor, but by 2010, all the women were observed being taken to the nearby hospital in Kunda village during labor.

In the village, some women would have a disease known locally as "Piryan." The tribesmen believed that Jinns were making the women sick and a few women were observed screaming, yelling, and shivering. The relatives of these women would bring them to the Mullah or a male relative who would proceed to beat the women saying that they were "hitting the Jinns" and not the woman. After being hit a few times, the women would calm down and the tribesmen proclaim that "the Jinns" left. These women with "Piryan" symptoms would also visit shrines or the Pirs in the area where the women would donate money and other goods to the Pirs and the custodians of the shrines in hopes of being cured, but by 2010, these practices had stopped for the most part. There were still known cases of women with "Piryans," but instances of the Mullah and the tribesmen beating the women when the "Jinns" arrived were not observed. Tablighi Jamaat was totally against this practice.

127

The Tablighi Jamaat members in the village do not appear to oppose girls' education. There is an elementary school for the girls in the village and some girls go to the elementary school, but don't pursue further any education. All of them get married and work at home as housewives since the women were not allowed to work outside the homes. Even the peasants' wives cannot work outside the home. The Purda (a total cover for women) was rigidly enforced by the males in village and this practice was consistent with the practices preached by the Salafists. On this issue, tension was not observed during studies in the village.

As noted earlier, the tribesmen were observed to be more religious than they were before the arrival of Salafism. It is important to understand that the Pashtun tribes have always been very religious and that Islam enjoys a special place among the Pashtuns. In the past, some tribesmen did not practice all the rituals, including praying five times a day in the mosque, but now the tribesmen were observed praying five times a day. Additionally, every tribesman must wash himself or herself before a prayer and they must change into clean clothes before prayers. This has improved the personal hygiene of the locals considerably, but the demand for washing forced the tribesmen to make arrangement for water at the mosque. Now the mosque contains a tube well, running water, cement washing places, and cement showers, and during winter hot water is available.

Salafism and Its Impact on the Tribal Structure

Tablighi Jamaat's Salafism phenomenon in the Pashtun area is unique when compared to other religious movements found in the Pashtun-inhabited areas of Pakistan and Afghanistan. Unlike previous movements that were let by the Mullahs or the Pirs, Salafism is led by the tribesmen themselves, who enjoy both religious and tribal legitimacy. These Salafist Amirs have both religious and tribal respect where in the past, the tribal leaders had tribal capital only while the Mullahs or the Pirs had religious capital. This distribution of power produced local social equilibrium, but occasionally the Mullahs would gain access to enough tribal power to wage jihad against an external enemy declared to be an "infidel." Once the jihad was over, tribal power would gradually gravitate back to the tribal leaders, creating equilibrium again in society, and a return to peace.

As explained previously, the Salafi movement is different because these Amirs, the leaders of this new movement, enjoy tremendous respect and power in the local communities. Frequently, these Amirs overplay their hand and attempt to use force to impose Salafism on their tribesman, and this has caused some backlash in other parts of the Pashtun area. Amir Gul Bahadar, in North Waziristan, is a both a legitimate tribal leader and a religious leader, but he has neither acquired a religious education nor he is a religious Mullah. The only religious credential he has that he is a Tablighi Jamaat Amir and that he is a Ghazi (a veteran of Afghan Jihad). Mangal Bagh in Khyber Agency is not a Mullah, but he enjoys similar tribal and religious legitimacy. Commander Nazir in South Waziristan Agency was a tribesman from the Kaka Khel Ahmadzai and a Tablighi Amir in the area, credentials that gave him both tribal and religious legitimacy. In Afghanistan, Mullah Baradar and Mullah Omar use Mullahs as part of their names, but they are not religious Mullahs in the traditional Pashtun sense. They are legitimate Pashtun tribesmen with legitimate tribal affiliation who use their tribal recognition and add their proclaimed religious recognition, which they acquired by waging jihad against a real or perceived "infidel." The Haqqani network operating in Afghanistan is very powerful because the Haqqanis enjoy both tribal and religious backing, but the Haqqanis are not Mullahs in the traditional Pashtun sense. A traditional Mullah is not normally a land-owning Pashtun leader. He is a custodian of a mosque who provides services to the tribe and in return he gets financial support from the tribesmen. The Haqqanis are legitimate tribesmen from Zadran tribe in Paktia Province of Afghanistan, but they are not perceived as Mullahs but since the Haqqanis claim both tribal and religious capital, they have emerged as a powerful foe of coalition forces in Afghanistan.

The phenomenon of Salafism could bring important change to the religious, political, social, and cultural structure of the tribes. Further, this phenomenon also appears to be permanent, not transitional, but this new movement may bring positive changes if it remains peaceful. However, it can get deadly as has happened in Swat, the FATA, and southern Afghanistan. Further, it becomes extremely difficult to roll back this movement because its roots exist deep within the tribal structure. The leaders of these movements are local tribesmen who are able to rally substantial parts of the tribe to their support, especially if they can make claims that Islam is being threatened

The political aspects of Salafism is different and the Amirs who have the legitimate claim to both traditional tribal and religious authority are likely to maintain leadership positions even after there is no justification for jihad in the area. The tribal elders will have a hard time reclaiming their original tribal position from these new leadership personalities. Ambitious Pashtuns always struggle to acquire leadership positions within their tribe and young men join the Mullahs to prove that they are brave and capable of attaining leadership positions. Once a jihad is over, some of these young men are recognized as legitimate tribal leaders and after they become tribal leaders, they have to compete with more entrenched, experienced tribal elders. The young men's leadership is tested in war, but their leadership is not tested in making peace, and in Pashtun society a leader's ability to unite families and the tribes in peaceful resolution of conflict translates into influence among the local tribesmen. The young men who acquire leadership due to jihad led by the Mullahs may or may not sustain or consolidate their newly found tribal authority because they lack experience in bringing peace to the local tribesmen.

The key to entering a senior leadership position among the Pashtuns involves an individual's ability to hold jirgas to bring peace to the tribe. Most of these young men, lacking any experience in managing jirgas, quickly lose the tribal gains acquired in a Mullah-sponsored jihad. In addition, Pashtun local tribal politics is very complex, dangerous, and demanding with local leaders walking a very fine line when it comes to sustaining their influence. Most of these young men who acquire leadership positions due to their participation in conflict or jihad are either murdered or neutralized because they don't have the necessary experience to deal with the complex, violent politics of Pashtun society.

These new Salafi Amir's participation in the jihad or in local tribal welfare activities serves to promote them to leadership positions while their rise in a tribe undermines the traditional tribal leaders that include the Khans, Nawabs, Maliks, and tribal elders. This also undercuts the religious leadership position of the Mullahs and the Pirs. Most Deobandi and Salafi Mullahs tend to extend support to the Amirs, further enhancing the religious legitimacy of the Amirs. Empowered with both tribal and religious authority, these Amirs emerge as powerful local tribal leaders and they are likely to remain powerful, even after the insurgency in Afghanistan ends. These Amirs are emotionally mature, politically calm, and the Tablighi Jamaat movement requires eight months of meditation training and an annual one month meditation program keep these Amirs calm and calculated in their decision-making. When in place and in control, they also enjoy the complete support of the local and regional religious leaders. Further, the maturity of their movement helps them manage local tribal dynamics effectively.

In the case of Pak Kaya village, Bilal and Hanif are the Tablighi Amirs. As mentioned previously, both are highly educated with college degrees. Both come from legitimate, powerful tribal families of the Jehangir Khel tribe and possess tribal authority that no one, including their elders in the families, can easily challenge. These two Amirs also acquired religious authority and they are recognized Amirs of the tribe in the area. On religious matters, the tribesmen look up to them, rather than to the local Mullah. The Mullah, who is a Deobandi, supports Bilal and Hanif, which further enhances their religious legitimacy. In other words both men are now extremely credible in the Jehangir Khel

Both Amirs extend mediating services to the tribesmen, expanding their tribal power even further while shrinking the tribal authority of the traditional tribal elders. This tribal and religious legitimacy have helped them to consolidate their influence within the Jehangir Khel and beyond Pak Kaya as well.

The long-term consequence of this shift from Sufism to Salafism may become destabilizing since the local governing institutions remain weak. The traditional tribal structure maintained order in the society, but as Salafism spreads among the tribesmen, it is likely to weaken the traditional tribal structure. The spread of Salafism will probably continue to undermine the role of the traditional tribal leaders and any weakening of the traditional tribal structure is likely to create chaos and disorder. Once this vacuum is created, the local Amirs will probably be tempted to come forward to act as stabilizers. This may happen in the village, but for now the traditional tribal structure at the village level is very strong and a portion of the tribe remains committed to traditional Sufism. The Tablighi Jamaat made inroads into the Jehangir Khel tribe, but they are still not in a position to dictate their practices as yet. Sufism and traditional tribal structure both remain relatively strong in the village and it will take few more years before the whole village turns toward Salafism, but at the current pace, the village may be totally Salafi in a short few years. It is hard to foretell the conditions under which these Amirs would resort to force to impose Salafism on the tribesmen as their peers are attempting in Swat or in FATA. For now, these Amirs and the Tablighi Jamaat are totally peaceful.

Tribal Gravitation to Salafism and Militancy

Serious questions arise then the relationship between the Pashtuns, the world's largest tribe, and extremism is considered. Among them: What is the future of these tribes as they gravitate toward Salafism? Are they going to be susceptible to the influence of religious currents championed by Al-Qa'ida and its allies who are using violent means to bring a political change in the Muslim world and beyond? What will it mean for the stability and security of the Pashtun-inhabited areas in Pakistan and Afghanistan? What does this mean for the stability of the governments in Pakistan and Afghanistan?

Recently the militants have been emboldened in the region due to the slow response, and in some cases, the lack of a response, by local governments. At times, the local governments appeased the Salafists by agreeing to their demands and these militant Amirs have challenged the writ of the states without any retribution. In some areas, the militants operate openly and even force the local people to donate money.

These newest Salafists have not created trouble for the locals and preach that jihad is an inner struggle and the local tribes appear to be flocking toward the Salafists because they don't have any other choice when formal and traditional governance is absent. Serious cleavages exist if one cousin supports the Tablighi Jamaat, the second cousin does not want to be left behind and often goes in the opposite direction. Everyone then starts contacting the senior leaders of the Tablighi Jamaat. Pashtun culture, however, cousins normally inherit enmity from their parents. Generally, it is hard to end this form of enmity and tribesmen get locked into a cycle of revenge. For example, if one cousin supports the Taliban or the Salafists, the other cousin would automatically do the opposite, triggering continuing competition and rivalry.

This is the undefined danger brought to the tribesmen by the transition from Sufism to Salafism that appears to be occurring. Realizing that this is a source of instability, the Taliban have been trying to end the local internal tribal or family enmities. They tell everyone that instead of pointing guns at each other, they should point guns toward the infidels in Afghanistan. The Salafists sometime force the locals to end their internal enmity, which is beneficial to all involved parties. The mediating services by the Salafists further enhance their prestige among the locals.

State institutions have struggled to deal with the issue of militants in the region but the military has generally retreated into their cantonments unless they are involved in large, coordinated offensives, leaving the civilians at the mercy of the militants. The police have been totally demoralized by the frequent suicide bombings by the militants while elites have been killed, forced out, or silenced. Many political leaders have retreated to Islamabad, Kabul, or other cities in Pakistan and Afghanistan. The senior Mullahs are too scared to speak out. They learned from the example of those who spoke out in the past and were killed by the militants. For example, Maulana Hasan Jan, one of the most respected clerics in the whole Pashtun area, was killed by the Taliban in broad daylight simply because he said that the suicide bombing was against Islam.

The intellectuals and the middle class are too afraid to speak out. Some of them have even joined the Salafists to save their family's interests. Even the more cosmopolitan "whiskey drinkers" either support Salafism or turn a blind eye toward the

Salafists' activities. Criminals, hashish smokers and heroin addicts who used to hang out in the hujra and ask for money to fulfill their habits, often join the local Taliban. Now, the drug addicts and common criminals are nowhere to be seen after they join the Taliban because it is more lucrative to work for the Taliban than for the landowners. Some militants kidnap rich businessmen for ransom. But the Tablighi Jamaat strictly prohibits its members from indulging in un-Islamic activities, including drug use and this allows young, troubled men to rebuild their lives.

In some areas the militants have used Tablighi Jamaat as cover, and have resorted to force, killing prominent local leaders. This may begin in this village. For example, the author lost two good friends to this kind of violence. Asfandyar Amir Zab, a prominent member of Swat's former ruling family and a former KP Education Minister, was killed in Swat in a bombing by the militants in 2008. Ahmed Khan Kuki Khel Afridi, a prominent member of Kuki Khel tribe in Khyber Agency, was killed in the summer of 2008 in the middle of the Jamrud bazaar near Peshawar.

As one local landlord recently confessed when asked the reasons why he might one day join the Taliban, "I get scared. I have been cooperating with the Taliban for a long time. How long can I do it, I don't know. You are so right. They are at my doorstep. There is nothing I can do about them. I don't have the army to confront them. I can't run away because I have no place to go to. Maybe one day I will have a beard and AK-47 like the Taliban. I may be a Taliban Amir due to my social status. This may be my only way out."

A Malik from South Waziristan Agency told a story in November 2009 about his family and how the Taliban made encroachments into his tribe. "My father was a powerful Malik in Wana, South Waziristan. He used to cooperate with the militants when they would show up at our hujra. He was doing it because we had an antagonistic relationship with the Toji Khel, a sub-tribe of Ahmadzai Wazir. We were Zilli Khel, a sub-tribe of Ahmadzai Wazir. We supported the militants because they were killing our enemies. When they finished killing the prominent Maliks of the Toji Khels, they turned their guns against my father. The militants made few attempts, but he survived the attacks. One day when he was coming home, he was ambushed and killed along with my two nephews and one uncle. Our family tried to confront the militants but we could not. We sought help from the Political Agent, but he refused to help us. We packed our belonging and moved to Peshawar. The Taliban are supported by our local services and the army. Commander Nazir, who killed my father, is supported by the Pakistani government. Our public can't do anything while the militants are supported by the government." This is a common view of villagers living in FATA.

An elder of Pak Kaya village told this story in November 2009: "You are relatively new to this society. In your years in the US, there have been many changes in the Pashtun society. There has been a great storm of fundamentalism sweeping across the valleys of the KP and FATA for the last two decades. This fundamentalism has been cross-fertilized by an influx of the jihadists from all over the world, bringing with them not only their narrow Wahhabi/Salafi ideology, but also sophisticated weapons, explosive expertise, and a distorted vision of Islam. The Pashtuns and their culture have been totally sidelined by these so-called Taliban jihadists. They don't have enough education and they don't listen to the educated religious scholars. A person spending over six months with Tablighi Jamaat, one of an Islamic proselytizing group in Pakistan can come home and claim to be a custodian of Islam. The government is not doing anything to confront these vigilante groups. The locals are too afraid to speak out. So, it has been very frustrating."

When the elder was challenged and asked: "Kaka (sir), if you continue to turn blind eyes toward what the Taliban is doing, and if the Pakistani government continues to believe that this problem would go away by itself, then who will solve this problem. The whole society has been destroyed; they are destroying Pashtun culture, heritage, and way of life. They are also destroying our next generation by prohibiting the girls to go to school and by recruiting the young as jihadists and suicide bombers. Don't you think we must do something?"

He continued, saying: "Listen, my boy, you are right, but this someone should not be you or me. The end game will be them killing you and me, which will bring shame and humiliation to our family. You have any idea what it means not to take revenge from this "illusionary enemy." Our family would be humiliated. No one will respect us because we would be unable to take revenge on the Taliban. Think about the cost, my son, to you, your family, and your whole tribe."

In Pashtun society, everyone must be perceived as strong and capable of taking revenge. A person who is incapable of taking revenge must submit himself to a relatively stronger Pashtun who is capable of taking revenge on his behalf. An alliance among the families and tribes is made to ensure the safety of each individual. Any transgression against any member of a family or a tribe or an alliance is met with revenge.

During a visit to the village in early fall 2010, the author met with a refugee from the Bajaur Agency. It appears that the Salafists and the Taliban used intimidation as a major tool to recruit the local tribesmen. He said, "The Taliban captured a young Afghan who was a butcher in his village in Bajaur. They slaughtered him like a chicken, even worse. Taliban alleged that he was spying for Afghanistan. It was just ruthless, Naka (Sir). They did it in such an inhuman way in front of everyone. Then, one Talib held the head of that poor man and displayed it to the crowd. Everyone there was scared. I am scared to death. There were about 10 of them on a pick-up truck. Some have AKs, others have RPGs. They were wearing jackets and covering their faces. They do not look local. They were not even talking to each other. They used sign language. They could be from anywhere. There was only one local person, the barber's son, Amir Saib. He was taking the lead. Everyone was so scared. After Taliban left, everyone was talking against them and their inhuman tactics."

The local tribesmen also use the Salafists to intimidate their rivals or to project their power. As one Malik from North Waziristan revealed in November 2009. "I used to have German shepherd dogs, four of them. I don't have them now and I don't need them because I have these Arabs and Uzbeks. They are my insurance. Nobody in this whole area messes with me. If anyone does, I just unleash these "German shepherds" against him. Trust me, they are ruthless. They slaughter people like we slaughter a chicken. The good news is that they are outsiders. They can do

139

whatever they want and can get away with it. We Pashtuns on the other hand have to worry about revenge. They don't."

When told that one day these militants would kill him, he responded "I know all this. I don't have any choice. At least I am buying time. If I don't support them and use them, my enemy will. I am walking on a very fine line. If I support the Taliban, which I do now, I buy time. Eventually, they may kill me or they may not. If I don't support them, my enemies will use them and get me killed. My father sided with British when they came to this area. Some people dubbed him as a traitor. I think he made the right decision and managed to protect his land and authority. I am doing exactly what my ancestors did for centuries. If the Americans show up tomorrow, and if I feel that they are going to vanquish the Taliban, I would be the first one to ditch the Taliban and support the Americans."

Accommodating outsiders has never been a problem in the area because there are always extra accommodations in every village. Every big Pashtun landlord owns and operates a big hujra. The size of the hujra determines a person's influence in an area. Some hujras consist of just a single room; others are five to ten room compounds. Anyone can stop by and spend the night. There are always beds in a hujra. The owner of a hujra feeds whoever shows up during mealtime. Every Pashtun tries to be perceived as hospitable and a person's ability and willingness to entertain guests determines his influence in the community. The poor segments of the society, who can't afford to use the hujra of a landowner. Sometimes in the rural areas, a whole sub-section of a tribe builds a common hujra, which functions like a community center. Most big landlords prefer to have their own hujra because the ownership of a hujra defines their power and prestige in the community. Peasants and other service providers including barbers, blacksmith, and drummers also use the landlord's hujra. They extend services to a landlord including entertaining a landlord's guests or cleaning his hujra and in return, the landlord opens up his hujra to them and their guests. Some landlords also provide free housing to the dependent classes.

The locals argue that extremism and the arrival of Salafism has something to do with the Pakistani policy toward the militants starting back in 1980 when Pakistan, in alliance with the US and Saudi Arabia, supported Afghan Mujahidin. As one elder noted, "This is all a product of Pakistani policy in 1980s. They developed this infrastructure of terror in the region. I think what is going on now is more than just fundamentalism. I think the Pashtun culture commonly known as Pashtunwali is giving way to Islam because the Pashtun culture has failed to address some of the issues in this fast changing society. Islam appears to provide a solution to the problems that Pashtunwali has failed to provide." For example, Pashtunwali demands an "eye for an eye" when it comes to revenge. In contrast, Islam stresses forgiveness. Pashtunwali requires hereditary leadership, but Islam facilitates achieved leadership. In Pashtunwali, the age of a person defines his influence and power, but in Islam age does not play an important role in leadership, giving younger men an opportunity to rise to leadership positions.

The Future of Salafism and Instability

The rising strength of the Salafists in the village may plunge the Jehangir Khel tribe into a violent internal struggle. It is possible that one day, tribesmen who follow Sufism could fight with the tribesmen who follow Salafism. This has

141

happened in other parts of the Pashtun inhabited area. For example, in Khyber Agency, two Afridi tribal groups, one following Sufism and the other following the Salafism, have been fighting with each other for several years. Due to this internal fight between Lashkar-i-Islam and Ansar-ul-Islam, all of Khyber Agency has been unstable. The government has not stepped in to mediate between the two groups and if either Al-Qa'ida or the Taliban decided to step in and successfully mediate between the two, the militants' prestige among the tribesmen would rise significantly. In addition, there is the danger that both groups may reach out to the Taliban and Al-Qa'ida for support, further strengthening the militants' position among the locals.

Once the cycle of violence starts, it becomes more difficult to stop it due to the mandatory revenge obligation under Pashtun culture. Even the local Mullahs have failed to mediate between the two groups in Khyber agency because the sectarian fight has turn into an internal tribal feud. It appears that the established Mullahs lost leverage over these local militant groups and these militant vigilante groups operating throughout the FATA and KP are not listening to anyone. This is a very dangerous situation that may replicate itself in Pak Kaya village where there is a clear division between the Sufis and the Salafists. The Amirs in the village are very assertive in their views. The Amirs don't listen to the local Mullahs because the latter are viewed as "disco Mullahs," implying that the Mullahs have sold out and are corrupt.

In the region, the author observed that the whole issue of terrorism has become a business and in Dara Adam Khel, for example, sophisticated weapons, suicide jackets, anti-aircraft guns, RPGs, explosive materials, Vehicle Born Explosives (VBIAD), and numerous other rocket launchers can be purchased. Worse, even suicide bombers are now sold in these incredible markets.

As one elder in March 2010 noted, "I am really worried about the future of the Pashtuns. I don't know how long it would take to put this genie of terror back into the bottle. Last time when the British fought against about 700 Hindustani fanatics, it took them over 60 years to push them to the Black Mountain areas. This extended period was needed even though the British were leading the fight and would bring in Sikhs and Gurkas, who were non-Muslims and who were as fanatical and as good warriors as the local Pashtuns. The British used to say that they matched fanaticism with fanaticism. Still, it took over 60 years to restore calm. How long will take this time, I don't know. Certainly, not in my life time."

Another elder joined in the conversation and said, "Doctor, welcome to Talibanistan. We got used to it. Look at me, it does not bother me to live in Talibanistan because I have a beard, I pray five times a day, I don't have any affairs with any women, I don't interact with females, except my sisters and wife, I don't listen to music. I don't have TV. I don't go to the movie theater. So I am already living like a perfect Talib or a Salafi. It is a problem for a person like you, who does not have beard, likes to interact with females, listen to music, like to watch movies, and occasionally pray or don't pray at all. If you live in Talibanistan, you have to live according to the rules of the Salafists."

The author asked the elder about the extent of the Pakistani government's writ. He responded, "Well, well, well.

Doctor, grow up and look around. There is no Pakistan here. If this is Pakistan, then why is everyone scared of the militants? Go dial "211" (Pakistani version of 911) or file a complaint in a police station against any Salafi militant. The Pakistani government has pretty much ceded its authority to these Taliban. The Taliban are the moral and religious vigilantes here on this side of the Indus River. As I told you, Doctor, everyone here acts like a Taliban. The Taliban moral and religious rules look rigid to you and to the thieves and criminals, the locals are happy or don't care much because the Taliban are bringing order to society, eliminating social crimes, purifying society from modern ills such as dirty DVDs and immorality. If the Pakistani government would have done its job, there was no need for these Taliban."

Likely Pakistani Policy toward the Salafists

Open source reports have indicated that the US and the West view Salafism, Al-Qa'ida and the Taliban as a threat to be eliminated, while Pakistan's policy toward the Salafists has been characterized as strategic recalcitrance. Sometimes, the policy is unclear and contradictory, according to local Pakistani analysts. Mohammad Safi, the host of Pakistan's Geo TV program in May 2013 noted that Islamabad has used force against some Salafi elements in the past, but it has also at times supported Salafists and a turned blind eye their activities. The Government of Pakistan, for example, took military action against the Red Mosque Salafists in Islamabad in 2007, and in 2010 the Pakistani military launched a series of military operations against Tehrik-I-Taliban in the FATA and KP, according to Safi. The Pakistani military also signed an agreement with some

Salafist groups in the FATA, including the Commander Nazir group in South Waziristan Agency and Hafiz Gul Bahadar's group in North Waziristan Agency, according to local Pakistani press reports. The Government of Pakistan condones the activities of the Tablighi Jamaat and its preaching in Pakistan because the Tablighi Jamaat apparently remains committed to its peaceful mission, according to Pakistani analysts.

It is widely reported in both local and international press that the Pakistani government supports the Afghan Taliban and their leadership and families continue to live in Pakistan. The Afghan Taliban appears to have social and religious depth within Pakistani society, along with the huge infrastructure of Salafi madrassas in Pakistan, according to local Pakistani press reports. The Afghan Taliban uses these madrassas and the mosques associated with them as recruiting and indoctrination places where they also raise money, according to academic studies.[53]

The Government of Pakistan's policy toward Salafist activities along the western border appears to be centered on the US presence, intentions and motivation in the region, according to Farah Taj, a Pakistani analyst based in Norway. She notes that Islamabad does not appear to view the militants' presence as a threat to Pakistani national security. Rather, Islamabad appears to view the Salafists' presence as beneficial to Pakistan's national interest. Most Pakistanis refer to Al-Qa'ida as "Al Fa'ida" (a thing that brings benefits) because the presence of Al-Qa'ida affiliated elements bring badly needed military and

---

[53] Girardef, Edward and Jonathan Walter, *Afghanistan*, Media Action International, Geneva, Switzerland. 2002.

145

financial aid to Pakistan, according to Bahdami, the host of an Urdu program, 11th Hour, on ARY TV.

Islamabad's unclear policy toward the Salafists in the region has created a trust deficit between Islamabad and Washington, according to Pakistani defence analysts. From these defence analysts' viewpoint, the US appears to believe that Islamabad is not sincere in its efforts to eliminate the militants' threat. Pakistani defence analysts note that Islamabad appears to believe that the US is using the threat of Al-Qa'ida as a pretext to station its troops in Afghanistan. Some elements within the Pakistani establishment even think that the US may one day use its forces stationed in Afghanistan against Pakistan or Iran.

The policymakers in Islamabad are divided into two main camps in their perception toward US involvement along the Pak-Afghan border, according to Pakistani analysts. This drives their lack of action against the militants and extremists. These analysts note one camp of Pakistani elites views the US presence in the region as a strategic opportunity, while the other views it as a strategic threat. The first group thinks that the US involvement in the region is a strategic opportunity because it is bringing Pakistan badly needed financial aid, long desired military weapons and technology, sought-after diplomatic attention on the world stage, and an opportunity to resolve the long-running dispute with India over Kashmir.

On the other hand, the second group views the US presence in the region a strategic threat to Pakistan, according to local Pakistani analysts. They think that the US presence in the region is not just to eliminate the militant threat, but they believe that the US has a secret agenda to redraw Pakistani borders and destabilize Pakistan to roll back its nuclear program. Some people in the Pakistani establishment think that the US, together with India and Afghanistan, would ultimately like to dismember Pakistan, according to Pakistani analysts. Following interviews of numerous Pakistanis, it seems that this paranoia about the US and the Indian threat to Pakistan appears to be driving Pakistan's behavior toward its western border.

For example, the first camp is reluctant to take serious action against the militants because they think if they eliminate the militants, the US would consider the threat resolved, and US forces would return home. They view the presence of militants as a strategic benefit because their presence keeps the US on the western border, bringing badly needed economic, political, and military dividends. This first camp is willing to tolerate an occasional blowback effect from militant activities because the cost of this potential blowback effect is less than the reward of militant presence in the area: the aid from the US, diplomatic recognition, and the flow of modern weapons to the Pakistani military.

The second group does not recommend taking action against the militants because they also think that the militants are their strategic assets, according to Pakistani defence analysts. This Pakistani camp thinks that these Salafi militants would be a force multiplier if and when the US (or India, Afghanistan) tries to destabilize Pakistan to get Pakistani strategic assets. This bifurcated view of Pakistan's situation regarding the multiple, but interrelated insurgencies occurring became obvious following my numerous visits to Pakistan over a decade.

Open source reports note that both Pakistani camps use different strategies to achieve their objectives. The first Pakistani camp continues to emphasize the strength of the militants in the region to the US and the West. They suggest that the Pakistani army lacks the counter insurgency capability needed to successfully take on this group. This camp also argues that widespread poverty in Pakistan is breeding militancy, that the militants are encroaching toward Islamabad, and that the root cause of the militancy is the Kashmir problem. This camp's purpose is to amplify the fear in the Western audience that there is a threat against their homeland emanating from the Pakistan-Afghanistan border, and that the Pakistani military is incapable of dealing with it. Therefore, the military needs help, to include more weapons and training. This camp including Ahmed Rashid, a well-known author, columnist, and the author of the book *Taliban*, also likes to emphasize the perception that the militants are getting closer to Islamabad, pointing out that if militants ever control Islamabad they would have control over the nuclear assets of Pakistan, posing a serious threat to the world.

The second camp also strategically markets its ideas about the militants' presence and their activities in Pakistan, and the US response to it to their domestic audience. This camp highlights the US drone attacks, numerous strings attached to US aid, the US media highlighting the militants' activities, the blowback effect of Pakistani support of US policy in the area, the US policy makers' criticism of the Pakistani army for "not doing enough," the US criticism of the Pakistani security services, and the US policy makers' public statements expressing concerns about the nuclear weapons falling into the hands of the militants.

Open source reports note that both Islamabad and Washington appear to read Pakistan's policy toward the Salafist militants differently, widening the wedge between the US and

Pakistan over how to handle the Salafist threat from Pakistan-Afghanistan western border. For example, the signing of Nazam-e-Adal in Swat by President Zardari in 2009 was seen by Islamabad as the right thing to do because it would remove one of the militants' rallying causes, helping Islamabad to create a wedge between the militants and the local population, according to local Pakistani analysts. The West, these analysts argue, viewed the signing of Nazam-e-Adal as a capitulation to the militant Salafists that would embolden the militants and consolidate their power in Swat.

The Kerry-Lugar aid bill passed by the US Congress in 2010 is also viewed differently by Islamabad and Washington, according to local Pakistani analysts. Washington added specific conditions to the aid to Pakistan, to ensure that Islamabad takes action against the militants, according to Pakistani defence analysts. However, Islamabad viewed the conditions as proof that the US does not trust Pakistan. The Pakistanis think that if the US is truly an ally, there should be no conditions on aid to Pakistan.

Islamabad appears to have no policy to contain, let alone reverse, the tide of the Salafism along the Pakistan-Afghanistan border, according to local and Western analysts. These analysts note that there are over 15,000 Salafist madrasas in Pakistan and most of these preach intolerance and a restrictive version of Salafism. The Pakistani government finances these madrasas through its Ministry of Religious Affairs, according to the analysts. In addition, the Pakistani secular schools are under-staffed, under-resourced, and poorly managed, according to the analysts, who further state that these schools have failed to liberalize the population.

Some Pakistani analysts note that Pakistani higher education appears to be fueling Salafism. As these case studies revealed, the college educated young men brought Salafism to the village, and college graduates have been acting as a vanguard of Salafism in the region. These analysts suggest that revamping the educational system and tailoring it toward the economic needs of society may stop this tide of Salafism. In addition, the analysts note that both Afghanistan and Pakistan need to improve their governance of militant activities. The analysts argue that unless and until the governments punish those who break the laws, the criminals and the militants will continue to flout the laws and impose their will on the locals.

Conclusion and Summary

Since the 1980s, different religious groups have been operating in the Pashtun tribal landscape of Pakistan and Afghanistan. Most of these groups follow Salafism. From more radical elements affiliated with Al-Qa'ida to the potentially feigned pacifist Tablighi Jamaat, all found followers among the Pashtun tribesmen. The principal tenet of Salafism is that the form of Islam that was preached by Muhammad and practiced by his Companions, as well as the second and third generations succeeding them, was pure, unadulterated, and, therefore, the ultimate authority for the interpretation of the two sources of revelation given to Muhammad, namely the Qur'an and the Sunnah [54]

I decided to use this small tribe and village as a case study for this book because there is a knowledge gap when it comes to micro-level analysis of the Pashtun area since most studies have analyzed the local militant and religious phenomena at a high strategic level. Since Pashtun tribes are fractured and decentralized, understanding the local tribal and village dynamics would help explain the phenomenon of extremism, fundamentalism, militancy, jihadist fervor, Al-Qa'ida's presence, the Tehrik-I Taliban and the Taliban insurgency in the area.

This study notes that there was equilibrium in a Pashtun society when the social, political, and religious capital was divided among the traditional leaders, the Mullahs, and the Pirs.

---

[54] Wiktorowicz, Quintan, "*Radical Islam Rising: Muslim Extremism in The West*," Lanham, Maryland: Rowman and Littlefield, 2005. *See* chapter 5 for information related to Salafism and their views of the Sunnah.

Since religious capital was split between the Pirs and the Mullahs, traditional Pashtun leaders enjoyed a dominant position since they maintained total control over the tribe.

The Pashtun tribes' gravitation from a traditional Sufi Sunni Islamic ideology to a new Salafi Sunni Islamic belief has fueled militancy, intolerance, extremism, and sectarianism in the area, potentially threatening regional and international stability. This transformation from Sufism to Salafism and resulting instability and militancy has impacted the local Pashtun tribes the most.

Basically, the Tablighi Jamaat Amirs want to transform the tribal way of life by undercutting tribal traditions and substituting their ideology. These Amirs believe that there are evils all around the Pashtun areas and that Pashtun society has been corrupted. From their point of view, the traditional tribal and religious leaders contribute to the social, political, and economic ills faced by the Pashtuns and the only way to cure all of these ills in the Pashtun society is the purification of the local society. The way to purify the local society involves the purification of the local tribesmen.

This research observes that the Tablighi Jamaat is bringing stability to the local tribal structure. As the traditional tribal society gives way to the forces of modernity, including modern communications, electronic media, access to cities and roads, modern education and a more modern economic sector, the Tablighi Jamaat and its Islamic practices appears to bring order to local society.

This study argues that this conversion from the Sufism to Salafism appears to be peaceful in certain Pashtun areas but violent in other areas. It is also argues that unless and until this conversion is managed by the local governments, the process may turn violent.

This research also shows that a conversion from a more tolerant Sufism to a more restricted Salafism would continue to transform local Pashtun tribal structure. It is argues that unlike in the past, where a transformation was temporary, the current changes appear to be permanent. This conversion from Sufism to Salafism is likely to restructure the Pashtun tribal structure, fueling internal strife and fissures within society. These internal fissures are likely to destabilize the local region, inviting to the local population more radical and violent Salafists including Al-Qa'ida.

This study also reveals what is happening within a Pashtun tribe, why it is happening, and why the local Pashtun tribesmen are gravitating toward these new religious groups. In addition it discusses the effects of this gravitation from the old Sufi religious practices to the new Salafi practices, describing the social, cultural, and economic outcomes of these changes. Are the changes manageable or are they generating tensions? Is this tension going to translate into a major tribal civil war as has been happening in the Afridi tribe in Khyber Agency? What is the outlook for the region for peace and prosperity, especially if they occur under al-Tabligh tutelage?

This Pashtun gravitation toward Salafism has been undermining the traditional tribal, social, and religious structure and this new movement has been changing the local tribesmen's life style. It could continue to undermine the local tribal structure and erode, and eventually destroy, the traditional tribal and religious leadership found among the Pashtuns. In the absence of

153

any other alternative, including modern governing institutions, such as security services and a judicial system, the Salafists are likely to fill the governance void as they did in some Pashtun inhabited parts of Afghanistan and Pakistan.

A closer look at this form of social change reveals that the shift from the traditional Sufi Islamic practices to this new Salafi Tablighi Jamaat practice has created divisions within the families that make up the Jehangir Khel tribe, at least for now. But Salafism is also bridging the divide among the local families which make up a Pashtun tribe, oddly bringing stability to the area.

EPILOGUE

Since late 2010, when the field research for this book was completed in Kaya village, new developments have occurred that may accelerate the Jehangir Khel tribe's shift from Sufism into the new, more extreme, Salafism. These new developments include a senior, powerful, elder joining Tablighi Jamaat, the creation of a Tablighi Jamaat women's cell in the village, and the announcement by a wealthy tribesman that he would donate land for the construction of a Salafi madrassa for the women in the village. These three developments may increase the pace of the Jehangir Khel's move from traditional Sufism toward Salafism and allow the Tablighi Jamaat to consolidate its gains in the region.

The villagers' attendance at the Tablighi Ijtama near Lahore, an enormous congregation of Tablighi Jamaat followers occurring every year in November has increased, according to a local tribesman. A local tribesman explained that in 2011 nearly all the people in the village attended the annual gathering and revealed that even Maan Khan, one of the stronger supporters of Sufism in the village, had converted and attended the gathering. Please recall that Maan Khan's son, Hanif, converted in the UK, and has been one of the senior Tablighi Jamaat Amirs in the village.

While Hanif was an Amir, his father Maan Khan, like most of Jehangir Khel elders, continued to support Sufism. When the local research for this book was conducted in 2010, Maan Khan and most of the Jehangir elders remained supporters of their Pirs and Sufism, and the accumulating data seemed to

155

predict that as the older generation died and a new generation of young men acquired additional responsibility and influence within their families, the whole tribe was likely to become Salafist. As previously explained, Shaid and Bilal converted their late grandfather, Hajji Yunus Khan, the patriarch of the Hajji family who was one of the most powerful and rich families in the tribe, to Tablighi Jamaat. Hajji Yunus converted to Salafism during his life, but his two younger brothers, Hajji Suilaman Khan and Hajji Ayub Khan, remained strong supporters of the Pirs and Sufism. Hajji Ayub Khan was also viewed as one of the pillars of Sufism in the village until he died in late 2010 and even his three children continued to support Sufism. Hajji Ayub Khan's oldest son, a retired Pakistani army Colonel, remains a strong supporter of Sufism.

The research showed that the Hajji family has generally shifted to Salafism with the 2010 death of Hajji Ayub Khan, the strong supporter of Sufism. Also, the conversion of one of Hajji Ayub's sons, the migration of Army Colonel Rafiq from Kaya village to Islamabad, and the declining influence of Hajji Suilaman Khan, whose children were all active members of Tablighi Jamaat, has nearly completed the shift of the Hajji family to Salafism. There are a few people from the Hajji family who remain supporters of Sufism, but their support appears to be based on "zad" (stubbornness, jealousy, or cousin's enmity) within an inter-family dispute rather than an ideological commitment to Sufism. Khalil, whose children were all active Tablighi Jamaat members by late 2011, remained a strong Sufism supporter, but Khalil has lost his influence and power within the family. Raham Zil Khan, a member of the Hajji family, also remains a Sufi supporter.

A local tribesman noted that Raham Dil Khan is now leading the Sufi group. Raham Zil Khan's support for Sufism is also based on personal considerations and is grounded in an interfamily rivalry. Rahman Dil Khan and Hajji Yunus Khan's families have had an antagonistic relationship for decades because Raham Dil Khan was once "allegedly engaged" to Hajji Yunus Khan's daughter. The "alleged engagement" was halted by the Hajji Yunus Khan family that later argued that the engagement had not been sealed properly and the daughter was subsequently married into another tribe. Since that incident, the families have not enjoyed a positive relationship. It is also interesting to note that Raham Dil Khan's nephews are all active members of the Tablighi Jamaat.

The second-most powerful family in the Jehangir Khel tribe is the Kabli family. As explained earlier, Hanif and his brothers and cousins were active Tablighi Jamaat supporters while Hanif's father, Maan Khan, and his uncles were active Sufi supporters. Maan Khan's conversion to Salafism certainly created a wedge among the senior elders of the Kabli family while his two remaining brothers, whose sons are active supporters of the Tablighi Jamaat, are getting older and losing their influence to their children. As these men age and as their sons assume more responsibly and gain additional influence, the Kabli family, still one of the most powerful families in the Jehangir Khel tribe, is likely to shift completely to Salafism. Once the Kabli and Hajji families shift away from Sufism, the whole of the Jehangir Khel will be a Salafist tribe.

Since 2010, another key development occurred in the village when for the first time the Jehangir Khel women became active in Tablighi Jamaat. The village women created a Tablighi

Jamaat cell that actively proselytized other women both inside and outside the village. This is a very interesting development because the Jehangir Khel tribe is one of the most rigid tribes in the region when it comes to restrictions placed and enforced on women. The women from the village, mainly the mothers and sisters of the Amirs, go on *Gusht* (a preaching assignment) for several days. These women, who in the past stayed home as housewives, are likely to assert themselves as their religious role expands, which is likely to accelerate the tribe's gravitation to Salafism.

There may also be positive aspects related to the women's emerging role in the Salafism movement. As these women expand their roles, they are likely to gain influence and power within the families that could empower them over the long term to speed development activities and openness in the region. These women may use Tablighi Jamaat as a platform to establish women's networks connected to different areas to further empower women who previously had been marginalized due to the restrictive nature of Pashtun culture and the tribal system. Once empowered, these women are likely to assert themselves within the family while also starting a process of shifting power within society. The women's cells could be used by Tablighi Jamaat to create awareness, and educate women in the region, which might free the women from the suffocating male-dominated Pashtun tribal system. However, there is the possibility that the women will start supporting radical leaders as the women in Swat did when they began to donate their jewelry to support Mullah Fazlullah, the Radio Mullah, in 2006 and 2007, according to the local press reports.

The women's role has expanded so much in Kaya village in approximately one year that Ismail Khan, Hajji Suilaman Khan's son who was one of the strongest supporters of Salafism, announced that he was donating of some of his land to support the construction of a women's madrassa in the village, according to a local tribesman. It was widely believed that Ismail Khan's decision was influenced by his mother, who was active in Tablighi Jamaat. The madrassa is to be built on the edge of the village and will only educate women. The creation of this Salafist madrassa is also likely to accelerate the tribe's shift into Salafism and may also undermine efforts by the Government of Pakistan to provide secular educations for the village girls. There is an elementary school for girls in the village, but instead of going to modern school, the girls are more likely to go to the proposed Salafist madrassa. This will also further increase illiteracy among the women while fueling additional extremism in the region.

There were only a handful of people left who remained supporters of Sufism, and they were weak within tribal family politics, according to a local tribesman. In addition, the Sufism supporters have been unable to recruit additional members; rather they have been losing supporters. For example, one of the remaining champions of Sufism is Lohar Sadiq, a member of the village's "dependent class". Sadiq and his family have been the *Lohar* (blacksmith) for the Jehangir Khel tribe for generations and while Sadiq is respected, he does not have influence in the tribe. Bajee Syed Ajmar Shah, whose brother and relatives are *Pirs*, is another active supporter of Sufism, but like Sadiq, Ajmar comes from a dependent family and does not possess power in internal tribal dynamics. In addition, Ajmar has a stake in preserving the old Sufi system that has rewarded his family for generations. Two other Sufi leaders, Raham Dil Khan and Khalil Khan, are full Jehangir Khel tribesmen, but their influence is both restricted and limited. In addition, both have been taking a lead in defending Sufism because of their *"zad"* rather than from a real commitment to Sufism.

The conclusion is obvious: the Jehangir Khel is likely to be a Salafist tribe quite soon. Fortunately, this shift from Sufism to Salafism has been a peaceful and evolutionary process so far and this peaceful trend may continue since the balance of tribal power has tilted so far in the favor of the Salafists that the Sufi supporters may not dare to resort to violence to prevent further Salafist encroachment on their faith. Since most of the powerful families have been either adopted Salafism or are gravitating towards it, the peaceful completion of this evolutionary process is likely. Additionally, the complete orientation of the tribe toward Salafism is probably unstoppable.

As Salafism takes a firm hold on the tribe, the consolidation phase will be interesting to observe. In other parts of the region, Salafists tend to overreach their actual power in their attempts to enforce their rigid interpretation of Islam. Tribesmen may tolerate orders by the Salafists, but this will occur only if these requirements or rules are viewed as anti-Sufism. If the Salafists attempt to enforce rules that seem to undermine local tribal dynamics, disturb the local power structure, or which challenge the local interpretation of Pashtunwali, the tribesmen may resent this and may very well rebel against the Salafists. This process has happened in other parts of the Pashtun inhabited areas in the region but for now, the Salafists' approach appears to be very accommodating and the Salafists have been tolerating numerous cultural practices that are normally prohibited by their interpretation of Islam. For example, villagers have continued to visit cemeteries and have continued to build cement shrines at gravesites, but the Salafists have not openly opposed this practice – yet. This trend toward Salafist practices may continue, possibly triggering resentment among the locals. If the Salafists start forcing each man to grow a certain style of beard or forbidding locals to play *Mokha*, a springtime archery game, and all the drums and dancing associated with it, they may meet with resistance from the tribesmen.

Major resistance is unlikely, even if the Salafists start overreaching, because the Salafist leaders come from powerful families of the tribe and the Amirs may now claim both religious and tribal strength, even undermining the power of the village's mullah. In other areas, Salafist leaders were outsiders and their movements failed because the Amirs of some of these Salafist movements were viewed as outsiders by the villagers. For example, Sayed Ahmed Shah of Bareilly and his fellow 19th Century Salafist Hindustani Fanatics failed in attempts to gain permanent Pashtun support for their religious movement because they were viewed as foreigners. Local Pashtun leaders opposed Sayed Ahmad Shah's movement at the time and these leaders sided against the Hindustani Fanatics, which resulted in their 1832 defeat at Balakot, near Mansehra, Pakistan. But now the religious and power dynamics within the village are different and the Salafist Amirs are local Pashtun tribesmen from the tribe's leading families, and Salafism was introduced by these same tribesmen. It would be difficult, if not impossible, to imagine a wedge emerging between the local tribesmen and these Salafists and their leaders, unless they attempt to take full secular control quickly instead of allowing it to happen through social evolution.

APPENDIX A: The Pashtun's Way of Life – *Pashtunwali*

The Pashtun are the largest ethnic group in Afghanistan, and the second largest ethnic group in Pakistan. Al-Qa'ida and the Taliban found safe haven in the Pashtun inhabited areas. Many people think that Pashtuns are a unique race with a peculiar way of life, Pashtunwali, which attracts the militants to their mix. Pashtuns and Pashtunwali are blamed for tolerating, and in some instances, encouraging the militants' activities in the area. What is it about the Pashtun way of life that appears to attract militants to their area? What are the different aspects of the Pashtun life which makes the Pashtuns prone to supporting the militants or militancy? What are different aspects of Pashtunwali that the militants exploit to find safe haven among the Pashtuns? How could the militants manipulate the Pashtuns and their culture to support their cause? Is there anything the world can do to drive a wedge between the Pashtuns and the militants?

Answers to these questions come down to understanding the mental impulse of a Pashtun, which would explain what drives a Pashtun to certain behavior or what motivates a Pashtun to act, either to extend support to the militants or to withdraw support from the militants. Understanding Pashtunwali may help end the militancy and extremism in Pakistan and Afghanistan. As Winston Churchill observed in the late 19th century, during the British expedition against the Pashtun rebellion led by the local Mullahs,

"I have been told that if a white man could grasp it fully, and were to understand their mental impulse—if he knew, when

163

it was their honour to stand by him, and when it was their honour to betray him; when they were bound to protect and when to kill him—he might, by judging his times and opportunities, pass safely from one end of the mountains to the other." [55]

It becomes very difficult to understand the concept of Pashtunwali for a person who is not a Pashtun because the definition of this concept varies from one region of Pashtun inhabited territory to another. Relying upon the explanation presented by local Pashtuns sometime carries a risk, too. The locals have a romantic view of the Pashtunwali concept, which taints their views and explanation of Pashtunwali to a non-Pashtun. The locals are prone to highlighting certain aspects of Pashtunwali that embody their personal feeling and views.

This research attempts to explain Pashtunwali. What are the different aspects of Pashtunwali? Why have the militants been successful in using Pashtunwali to find safe heavens? What should the world do to understand this concept? This study will use a series of case studies in Pak Kaya village in the Pashtun area to make the point that Pashtunwali is a complex concept that captures different aspects of a Pashtun's life.

An Ideal Pashtun

The key to understanding Pashtunwali is to understand the Pashtuns' notion of "an ideal man." Every Pashtun wants to be a Pashtun, which means a Gahyaratmand Pashtun, an ideal

---

[55] Churchill, Winston S., "The story of the Malakand Field Force," p. 20.

Pashtun who embodies "Pakhto", or leading a totally honorable life. An ideal Pashtun is a person who embodies the spirit of the Pakhto. This means the ideal Gahyaratmand Pashtun is tuhrawala (courageous), hayadar (respectable), sateetob (humane), rahamdel (merciful), bahadar (brave), mahmannawaz, (hospitable), khandani, (a descendent from honorable ancestors), and deendar (religious). All these are the components of Pashtunwali, which a Pashtun must follow to live as a Gahyaratmand Pashtun.

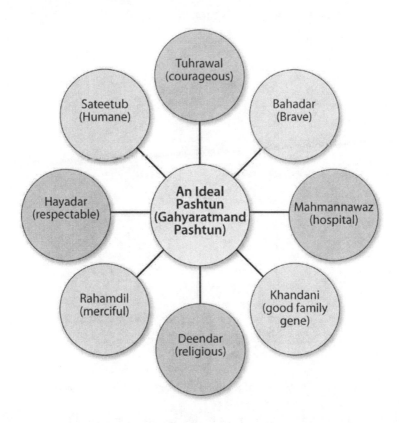

Figure 12. Characteristics of an Ideal Pashtun.

An Ideal Pashtun and Pashtunwali

Every Pashtun strives to be an ideal Pashtun who embodies the characteristics defined by Pashtunwali. In order to develop these characteristics, a Pashtun has to live a certain lifestyle in order to be perceived as a Gahyaratmand Pashtun. A Gahyaratmand Pashtun has to prove to his fellow Pashtuns that he is willing and capable of following an ideal Pashtun way of life. If a person follows Pashtunwali, he is praised as a Gahyaratmand Pashtun. However, if a person doesn't follow the tenets of Pashtunwali, he is paigored (reproached) as bagarat (a man without an honor).

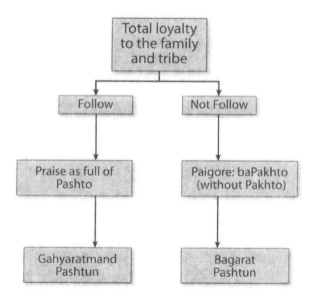

Figure 13. Process of Shaping an Ideal Pashtun – or Failing.

A Gahyaratmand Pashtun has to be viewed as Tuhrawal, or courageous. In times of war or conflict, when his family is attacked, or a tribe goes to war against a rival tribe, a Pashtun

166

may be required to prove his Tuhra. Sometimes, people show Tuhrawal by resolving a conflict between two families, or by achieving a special place in society, or by successfully standing up to a bully. Tuhrawal covers different aspects ranging from successfully prosecuting a war to an ability to take revenge on behalf of his family or a tribe to a capability to make peace to achieving a special place in a society. For example, the locals view a Pashtun as Tuhrahala if he devotes his resources to help someone or if someone leads a Lashkar if the tribe wages a war or if someone rescues someone from a difficult situation or shows heroism. The key is that a Pashtun should be perceived as Tuhrahala by his fellow tribesmen.

Pashtunwali and Bahadar (Bravery)

A Pashtun has to be seen as brave and resists any attempt by another to denigrate his reputation as a brave man. A Pashtun, for example, prefers to become a Ghazi (a veteran of a holy war) rather than a martyr. He uses his credential as a Ghazi to claim prestige and power among his fellow tribesmen. This quality also requires that a Pashtun is capable of behaving ruthlessly towards his enemy. He has to be seen as brave enough to take revenge if and when there is an attack on his honor or if and when there is physical attack against him or his family or tribe. Fighting on behalf of one's relatives and friends is another requirement of a brave Pashtun.

Tribesmen view a Pashtun as Bahadar if he or she does something extraordinary. Showing heroism or showing extraordinary strength is a sign of bravery. For example, a young man grabbing a bull and pulling it to the ground is perceived as brave. A man standing up to a bully or a Badmash (trouble maker) is viewed as a sign of his bravery. A man extending a loan to someone in his tribe or to a needy relative is perceived as brave. A man is viewed as Nar (brave) if he takes the lead when there is a Hashar (a tribal collective effort to complete a task or a community uniting to finish a task—cutting grass in common land or helping a tribesman to put a roof on his house or the young men digging a graveyard when someone dies.)

A woman raising a child and sending this child to avenge the death of her husband is seen as a sign of bravery by the society. A widow raising her children without getting remarried is viewed as a sign of bravery. A woman showing modesty in her clothing and ensuring Purdah (head to toe cover) is considered to be demonstrating an act of bravery. A woman enduring a pain of living among abusive in-laws, rather than divorcing her husband, is viewed as brave woman who never left her family to return to her father's house.

A Pashtun who is perceived as Yaradunka (fearful) never acquires respect among the tribesmen. A Pashtun tries to resist, even fight, any attempt to denigrate him as Yaradunka.

Sometimes, standing up to a powerful enemy and getting a beating is seen as a sign of Bahadary. In other words, a person does not have to win a fight to become a brave. A person may lose, but still perceived as brave. So, standing up against a powerful enemy and fighting to the end is viewed as a sign of bravery. Facing an enemy is also a sign of bravery. The Taliban in Afghanistan are seen as brave because they have been fighting against the all-powerful US and the coalition forces. The average tribesman thinks that the Taliban are brave because although they have been taking the beating, they have been fighting against a powerful enemy. The Arabs, who are fighting alongside the Taliban, are perceived as brave because they left their families and comfort of their lives and to travel to Afghanistan and Pakistan to wage a jihad.

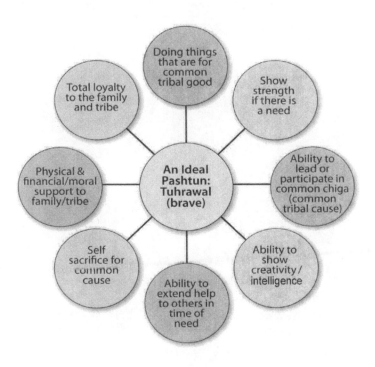

Figure 14. Characteristics of a Brave Ideal Pashtun.

Time is irrelevant in Pashtun culture and a tribesman may take years before they attack their enemy or before they avenge the killing of a family member. There is a saying among the Pashtuns that "if a Pashtun avenges the death of his loved one in one hundred years, it is still too soon."

In Pashtun culture, the end justifies the means. The locals do not care how a person avenges the killing of his loved one. A person does not have to attack his enemy head on. He can hide in the bushes and attack his enemy. There is a saying among the Pashtun that a person figures out first how to sneak out of a place before he chooses a launching place for an attack. With this in mind, it is not surprising that the Taliban in Afghanistan use IEDs against coalition forces.

Figure 15. Characteristics of a Coward among Pashtuns.

Pashtun culture requires that a strong person practices Tepose (inquiring about the wellbeing of someone). A person is expected to inquire about the health of sick and elderly. He is expected to attend the sick even if the ill person is from a poor family. He is also expected to attend the funeral of everyone, including a poor person and to   visit the deceased's family and express condolences.

Pashtunwali and Malmastia (Hospitality)

One of the tenets of Pashtunwali is Malmastia (hospitality). A Pashtun must be seen as a hospitable. This characteristic enhances a Pashtun's power and prestige among the tribesmen. The farther a Pashtun spreads his dastarkhawan (food mat), the more respected he is. Hospitality is used by the Pashtuns to enhance their power and standing in the community. A Pashtun has to own a hujra, and has to keep it open continuously to show that he is hospitable. If someone comes to his hujra, he has to provide free lodging and food to this person. If a Pashtun can't afford to have a hujra, he has to join the rest of his relatives and built a joint hujra. The quality of hospitality is used by every Pashtun to signal to his friends and relatives that he is capable of taking care of them if and when there is a need, and a signal to his enemies that he can afford to feed and house people if there is a need for hospitality. This hospitality also demands that a Pashtun has to show mercy to his enemy if the latter shows up at his doorstep. By forgiving his enemy, he shows magnanimity and grace, which enhances his power and prestige. The Pashtun culture is not designed to punish an aggressor but to address the grievances of the victims in order to prevent further conflict.

A Pashtun also expects to be treated fairly and respectfully when he visits someone's house. Any discrimination is met with resentment and anger by a Pashtun. A Pashtun is offended when he is told that "I don't have time" or "I am busy, come, please some other time." He feels that he has not been extended hospitality.

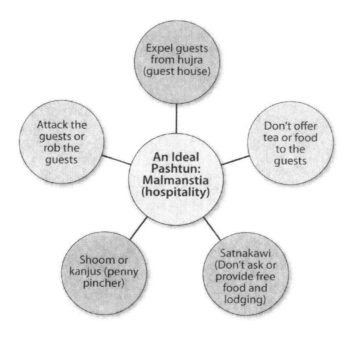

Figure 16. Pashtun Hospitality.

Pashtunwali and Deendar (Religiousness)

A Gahyaratmand Pashtun always wants to be perceived as a religious person and a defender of Islam. Most Pashtuns proudly claim that there is no non-Muslim among Pashtuns. The appearance of being a religious man is more important than actually being religious. He is expected to respect religious clerics and faqirs (ascetic holy men).

A Pashtun does not want to become a martyr. However, if he does, his family members use his martyrdom to enhance their power and respect. Pashtuns prefer to become a Ghazi and participates in a holy war in order to be seen as religious and brave. He fights in a holy war with the sole intention of surviving the conflict and returning home as a Ghazi. A Pashtun donates money and other material to a jihad because he wants to be seen as pro-religious.

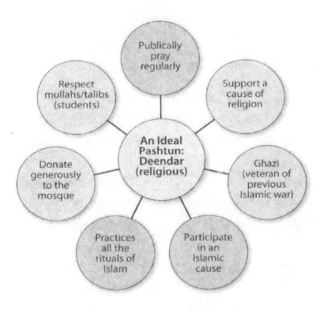

Figure 17. Aspects of Religion for a Pashtun.

Pashtuns respect clerics and religious students (Taliban) but they also look down upon them. The clerics are referred to as "moolyan" and the Taliban are called "chanrah," both derogatory terms in Pashto. A landowning Pashtun normally does not marry into a Mullah's family. This has been begun to change among the Afghan Pashtuns, where there are a larger number of Mullahs who gained prestige, power, and money in the 1980s.

A Pashtun is very superstitious when it comes to religion. For example, he never points his toes toward the Kaba, the holy shrine in Saudi Arabia. When Pashtuns travel on the Hajj, they follow special rituals upon departure and arrival. In addition, special signs are displayed to show how important the Hajj is for the Pashtuns.

Pashtunwali and Rehamdil (Forgiveness)

A Pashtun is expected to be brave but merciful and forgiving. The perception of an individual Pashtun being a merciful and forgiving enhances his influence and respect. A Pashtun is expected to show mercy to the perceived weaker elements of society, including children, the elderly, and women. He is also expected to show mercy to a weak person, even a weak enemy. A Pashtun who does not show mercy is perceived as "Zalam" (cruel). The Pashtuns like bravery but dislike cruelity. For example, a Pashtun is expected not to kill children or female relatives of his enemy. If an enemy surrenders (Nanawata), a Pashtun is expected to show mercy and he is expected to forgive the enemy.

Tehrik-i-Taliban and other militants in the FATA and KP have lost their credibility because they are perceived as "Zalam." The TTP's tactics are perceived as inhuman and cruel, because they have been involved in the killing of innocent, powerless tribesmen.

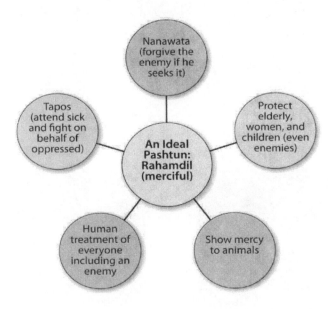

Figure 18. Aspects of Mercy in Pashtunwali.

A Pashtun is also expected to treat animals kindly. He is expected to feed his animals and take good care of them. He is also expected to kill animals in a humane way.

Pashtunwali and Sateetob (Civility and Honesty)

A Pashtun is expected to show respect to elderly and women in public. He is expected to dress modestly and conservatively. A Pashtun who is flashy or vulgar is perceived as "dom" (a dancer...a reproach in Pashtun culture). A woman who does not dress conservatively is labeled as "Kanjri" (or dancer). She is also viewed as an immoral woman.

A Pashtun is expected to cover himself in front of other people and expects others to show modesty as well.

Figure 19. Pashtunwali Requirements for respectability.

A Pashtun is expected not to humiliate another human being in public. Humiliating a Pashtun in public is met with resentment, and can bring about possible revenge. For example, the Taliban have been dyeing criminals black and parading them in public on donkeys. The Taliban have been using this method to prevent other people from committing the same crimes. A Pashtun punished like this must leave that area and settle somewhere else because he lost his honor. His other option involves taking revenge by going after the Taliban.

A Pashtun is expected to show respect for women. He is expected not to look straight into the face of women. He is also expected to protect women if they are threatened by someone. The police are not expected to search women.

In addition, a woman is expected not to act like a tomboy. She is expected to show modesty and is expected to stay at home. Outside the home, she is expected to cover herself, including her face. A man allowing his female relatives to leave the house without proper "Purdah" (cover) is perceived to be Bagayrat. A Pashtun loses his respect and influence in his community if he is perceived as being "liberal" in his attitude toward women.

The women who do not live according to the norms of Pashtunwali are perceived as "challo," meaning that they have bad character. She and her family completely lose respect and honor in Pashtun society.

Death of a Tribesman and Pashtunwali

The following case studies further explain Pashtunwali. As noted earlier, Pashtunwali is a complex concept. Pashtuns use events in their daily lives either to neutralize their enemies or to gain respect in the local communities. As explained previously, the Salafists have been relatively flexible when it comes to combining Salafism with Pashtunwali. Despite the differences between Islam and Pashtunwali, the Salafists have managed to make inroads into the closed Pashtun tribal society. Tablighi Jamaat's organizational structure and its flexibility have been the keys to their success.

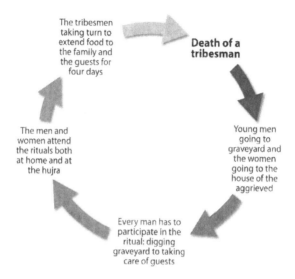

The tribesmen taking turn to extend food to the family and the guests for four days

Death of a tribesman

Young men going to graveyard and the women going to the house of the aggrieved

The men and women attend the rituals both at home and at the hujra

Every man has to participate in the ritual: digging graveyard to taking care of guests

Figure 20. Pashtunwali Requirements for Funerals.

Case Study: On August 13, 1993 a son of Khursheed Khan died and an announcement of the death was made on the Mosque loudspeaker. The women gathered at the Khursheed house while the men gathered at the hujra. The young men picked up the necessary materials from the hujra and went to the graveyard where they dug the grave. The funeral was held at 2 pm and men from both the Pashtun families and the dependent class families participated in the process. The village moalana, Mustafa, led the prayer. After the prayer, the body was buried by the village elders. All the men retreated to the hujra. The men from the dependent classes, especially the younger men, waited on people, including guests from outside the village. Tea was provided by the Yunus Khan family. During the next few days after the death, the older men in the village stayed at the hujra and received guests. The ceremony continued for four days. On the first day, the Yunus Khan family provided food and tea to the guests and the family of Khursheed Khan. The next day, the Tamraz Khan family provided food. On the third day, the Maneera Khan family provided food. On the fourth day, the Sham Dar Khan family provided food. The ceremony ended on the fifth day.

Every person in the village participates in this type of event. It is requirement of Pashtunwali to attend a funeral. In this example, the women went to the house and the men went to the hujra to express condolences and to participate in the rituals. Tribesmen are expected to take care of incoming guests and their food and lodging. In this case, a public call went out from the mosque loudspeaker and every young man who was capable of physical labor was observed walking toward the graveyard. One man from every family is required to be present while the grave is dug.

The older men are required to be present at a hujra for three days. Every man at the graveyard shows his Tuhrawali by helping dig the grave while the entire Jehangir Khel tribe participated in the event to show their solidarity with the aggrieved family. In an event like death, all members of the Jehangir Khel set aside their differences to participate in the event. There are rare instances where two families have a blood feud and they don't attend each other's funerals. The women who go to the house for Tapos (to show grief) also demonstrate Pashtunwali. At least one woman from each house is required to be at the aggrieved family's side for three days. At night, the women can go back home and spend the night but during the day at least one woman from each household is expected to be present. If no one shows up, the local people call that family "Ba Pakhto."

As this section shows, an event like a death in a tribe provides an opportunity to every tribesman to show his Pashtunwali. Each tribesman can demonstrate his or her Pashtunwali by participating in certain rituals and by doing certain kind of chores expected from him. A tribesman's participation in a funeral shows his support to the aggrieved family, as well as his religiousness. By sharing the physical and financial burden with the aggrieved family, a tribesman shows that he is merciful, respectful, kind, and loyal to his fellow tribesmen. By helping dig the grave, a young man shows his strength and commitment to the village.

Marriage and Pashtunwali

This section explains how Pashtunwali is involved when someone in the village gets married. The entire village participates in the arrangements for the wedding. Food preparation and receiving and accommodating guests are activities shared by all of the villagers. The guests are served first; then the villagers. Accommodating overnight guests is shared collectively by all the villagers. During the entire process, both Pashtuns and the dependent classes participate in various parts of the ceremony.

Each person in the village feels included in the celebration. The villagers provide free labor. In some cases, a loan is provided to the groom's family. In the barat (going to the bride's home and bringing her and the giaze[56] back to the

---

[56] The bride's wedding party.

groom's household) the owners of the vehicles in the village provide free transportation. Each person is given an opportunity to demonstrate his or her connection to Pashtunwali. The young men extend labor in order to show their commitment to the family of the groom or bride while the older people simply show up and participate in the rituals.

Case Study: Shahzada, a younger brother of Dost Mohammad, was married on August 15, 1993. At about 5pm on August 5, Mohlah Bakhsh informed the Jirga members of the time, venue, and purpose of the Jirga. Dost Mohammad convened the Jirga, which had a total of thirty participants. Two religious households were represented by Mohammad Omer and Mustafa. The other twenty-eight members were Pashtuns, each representing his family. During the Jirga, Shah Gul and Abdullah, two members from the dependent classes, made seating arrangements, and provided water, and Chelum (traditional smoking) service. A few members from the dependent classes, and some of the younger members of the village, sat in the back seats and listened to the Jirga.

Dost Mohammad started the proceeding by telling the members about the proposed marriage of his brother. He also noted that Tamraz Khan's family had boycotted the Jirga. He formally announced the date of the marriage and the number of guests to be expected. After his brief introductory remarks, Yunus Khan, an older man from the Haji family, requested that the Jirga mediate between the Tamraz Khan family and the Dost Mohammad family. A committee was formed consisting of Mustafa (a religious moalana), Yunus Khan, Mir Akbar Khan and Atham Khan.

A general discussion took place. Some members suggested that the food preparation should take place at Yunus Khan's hujra because it was closer to the house of the groom's family. Other suggested Khan Mohammad's house. After deliberation, it was decided to prepare food at Khan Mohammad's house.

The discussion on logistics and food lasted for an hour. Each person participated in the discussion. The older members were observed talking more as compared to the younger ones. After about two hours of deliberation, the Jirga ended its session. The following steps were taken by the Jirga:

First, a committee was formed to mediate between Tamraz Khan's family and Dost Mohammad's family. Second, the date of the marriage was approved. Third, the Jirga members gave their full assurance of help and cooperation. And finally, a consensus was developed concerning the place where cooking would take place and how the food would be served.

Immediately after the Jirga, the mediation committee went into session. They outlined the strategy for the mediation process. It was decided that Yunus Khan would establish contact with Tamraz Khan and his brothers Man Khan and Khawas Khan. After the initial contact was made, a meeting would be held and Dost Mohammad would be called into the meeting, if necessary. After the committee's meeting, Yunus Khan contacted Tamraz Khan and talked with him in private. The meeting lasted about thirty minutes in which Yunus Khan asked about the specific grievances the Tamraz Khan family might have toward the Dost Mohammad family. Tamraz Khan spelled out some grievances related to the dispute between the two families over a piece of land. After the discussion, Tamraz Khan agreed to participate in the wedding, provided his brothers agreed.

After the meeting, Yunus Khan contacted Man Khan. A meeting was held at Man Khan's house at about 10pm. After a few minutes, Man Khan's brother, Khawas Khan also came and attended the meeting. The meeting lasted about 45 minutes, and both Man Khan and Khawas Khan agreed to participate in the wedding. Then, a meeting was called for the following day at about 6pm at the hujra. Only Tamraz Khan, Khawas Khan, Man Khan, Dost Mohammad, Yunus Khan, Atham Khan, and Mir Akber Khan participated in the meeting. The Jirga started with a simple statement by Yunus Khan. He said to Tamraz Khan and his brothers, "Please forget about the past, and come and participate in the happiness of Dost Mohammad's family."

Tamraz Khan, in turn said, "We will participate and don't have anything against the Dost Mohammad family." Then, a general discussion took place about the wedding arrangements.

A few days before the actual marriage ceremony, various preliminary activities started. Dost Mohammad sent Mohlah Bakhsh, a Dum, to inform his friends and relatives of the impending ceremony. Zarat, a Nai, went to inform people in nearby villages. A few older members of the Jirga including Yunus Khan, Tamraz Khan, Mir Akber and Atham Khan went as a delegation to Ethli Kaya, another village. They went from hujra to hujra and invited the people for the wedding lunch, called the Walima.

Three days before the formal marriage ceremony, the activities started. All the people in village were observed taking an active part in the arrangements. The young people helped bring wood from the forest located a couple of miles from the village. Others helped in moving furniture. One night before the marriage, after the evening prayer, older men, one from each Pashtun household, were invited by Dost Mohammad. In the presence of these people, three animals were slaughtered, at which point the formal wedding started. The young men helped in slaughtering animals and preparing meals. The younger men prepared bread and installed Shamyanas (tents).

A lot of activities were going on inside the houses. Dost Mohammad's mother and sisters invited the women to their house. One night before the wedding, almost all of the women in the village participated in the ceremony called Mandhee. The women went to the bride's home with all of the traditional clothes and gifts. The women from the village were observed helping the groom's family in the cultural and religious parts of the ceremony.

The dependent classes also participated in the wedding. They made the necessary arrangements for the incoming guests. The women from the dependent classes helped the groom's family inside the home. The men were seen helping the groom's family with tasks outside the house. It was interesting to see how the groom's family saved money by using the free labor provided by the community. Some people even contributed wheat and rice which saved the groom's family more money.

On the day of the marriage, the wedding lunch was served from 10am to 2pm. All the village men, especially the younger ones, served the guests. In addition, the village women served the women guests inside the home. The entire community was involved in serving the meal.

After the lunch, at 4pm, all the men in the village and the male guests went to the bride's home located in Uthli Kaya, about a half mile from the village. Upon their arrival they were received by the bride's family and relatives, and they were served tea and other refreshments. After the necessary cultural and religious events, at about 6pm, the men from the community came back with the dowry and the bride. Some men from the bride's family accompanied the bride. Upon their arrival in Terli Kaya, they were served dinner by the groom's family. After this event, leftover food was distributed among the people. The community helped in cleaning up after the meals.

This section reveals that an event like a marriage provides an opportunity for a tribesman to demonstrate his connection to Pashtunwali's traditions. The young men are expected to help cook the food. They are expected to entertain the guests before they eat the food. The women are expected to visit the groom's house and participate in the rituals. The women are expected to share all of the marriage with the groom's family. The older men are expected to attend the event without doing physical labor. Right before the meal starts, all the older men, led by the village Mullah, are expected to visit the cooking site and offer prayers. With these prayers, the formalities begin. The tribesmen show their kindness, hospitality, and respect to the guests.

Village Unity and Pashtunwali

In this section unity and cooperation in the village will be discussed through some examples of how the tribesmen demonstrate their Pashtunwali. In addition, the process and method of conflict resolution are also discussed. This section reveals that both young and old demonstrate their bravery and leadership during the whole process of reconciliation.

Conflict Resolution

The village has developed very effective methods of conflict resolution. Most conflicts arise due to water distribution, land claims, and children's disagreements. The Jirga is the main instrument of conflict resolution. I observed two kinds of conflicts in the village -- minor conflicts and serious conflicts.

Minor Conflict

A minor conflict involves two people attacking one another physically or verbally. After the fight, a Jirga is called. Any senior member of the community can call the Jirga. The Jirga invites the two parties to attend and speak. The Jirga defines the root cause of the fight and then places the responsibility on one party. In most cases, the Jirga mediates between the two parties and settles the dispute without blaming either party in the dispute through a consensus decision that normally effectively halts the dispute.

Case Study: On May 1992, a son of Khawas Khan and a son of Chan Mobarak, had a fight in the hujra. Both boys were slightly injured. The uncle of Chan Mobarak's son, Bahadar Khan, was present at the time. He came and sided with his nephew. This complicated the situation. The emotions ran very high among the Khawas Khan family. Khawas Khan's family got together at his house and decided to take revenge against the other family. In this case, Bahadar Khan sided with his nephew to show his bravery by siding with his family's member without determining if his nephew was right or wrong. In contrast, Khawas Khan's family rallied behind his son.

Upon receiving the news, Yunus Khan came to the hujra and contacted Karam Khan, an older respected man from the Mani Khal family. Both men went to the Khawas Khan house and met with the elders of his family. Here again, both Karam Khan and Yunus Khan were demonstrating their Pashtunwali by defusing the situation. A senior leader in a tribe demonstrates his leadership by restoring peace. At first, both received a cool response from the family of Khawas Khan. After about two hours of deliberation and heated conversation, Khawas Khan and his brother Man Khan agreed to attend the Jirga which would discuss the issue.

The Jirga went into session at about 6:15pm at the hujra. First, Karam Khan described the event in a very conciliatory tone. He urged both families to forget about what he called "children's fighting" and the mistake by Bahadar Khan in taking one child's side. Then, Khawas Khan condemned Bahadar Khan's action. After his remarks, a general discussion took place. After about one and a half hours, both parties agreed to settle the dispute. Bahadar Khan's family apologized for what had happened. The dispute was settled peacefully without any further incident.

In this example, different tribesmen had an opportunity to demonstrate their Pashtunwali. Bahadar Khan quickly joined the fight because he was trying to show his bravery, but in the end his action was condemned. He apologized for his involvement because as a relatively older man, he should have separated the boys. Bahadar Khan should have shown kindness in the matter rather than joining the fight. Both Karam Khan and Yunus Khan demonstrated their Pashtunwali by mediating between the two parties. A successful mediation by these two elders further enhanced their status. They were perceived as kind, respectable, and courageous to undertake such the process of conflict resolution. Their ability to hold a jirga and end the conflict further enhanced their reputation and leadership.

Serious Crime

If a tribesman kills another person, the village Jirga would resolve the matter. It uses various mechanisms.

First, a Jirga asks both parties to forgive each other.

Second, the Jirga recognizes that it is not simple to forgive the killing of one's family member(s). A grand Jirga consisting of respected people from the village and from other villages assembles and solves the problem by a kind of remuneration system. A victim's family receives Sora, i.e. the victim's family is given a girl from the offender's family in marriage in order to compensate for the loss of life. This Sora establishes an on-going familial relationship between the two families, which in turn, helps heal the wounds caused by the killing. In certain cases, the Jirga expels the family with the murderer from the village, and asks the aggressor's family to leave as well.

Case Study: The village faced only one situation where a young man, Mehdi Khan, son of Fareed Khan, killed a poor farmer in 1990. As background, Mehdi Khan became involved in more criminal activities after joining a big criminal gang in Zaida. He and his gang were involved in a series of killings in the area, but he did not commit any crime in Pak Kaya. However he would come at night and harass young men in the village.

One day, he harassed a young man from a very poor dependent class in the village. The young boy's older brother met with Hattam Khan, an older man who often participated in the Jirga. Hattam Khan called an emergency session at 7:pm after the prayer time at the hujra. He explained the incident and drew the attention of the Jirga to Mehdi Khan's activities. The Jirga, after discussing a series of options, decided to bar Mehdi Khan from the village. They decided to kill him if he came to the village. Mehdi Khan's father was dead so his older brother, Meer Sultan, was invited to the Jirga. Meer Sultan was told about the decision of the Jirga. He was also told to leave the village if he and his family could not accept the decision of the Jirga. The following day, Meer Sultan and his family left the village and migrated to another area.

This example tested the Pashtunwali of numerous tribesmen. The Jehangir Khel stood up to Mehdi Khan and his gang. This action showed their bravery. In addition, the Jehangir Khel tribe stood behind a poor man against Mehdi Khan's family, which was a Pashtun family. Mehdi Khan was from a dependent family of Musa Khel. The young boy who was harassed was from the weaver's family. The Jehangir Khel elders depended on the weaver's family and made a united stand. This shows the Pashtunwali of the leaders of the Jehangir Khel.

189

The elders showed kindness and mercy to the poor boy who was harassed by Mehdi khan and his gang. The Jehangir Khel also demonstrated bravery when they stood united against an outlaw—Mehdi Khan.

Meer Sultan stood by his brother even though Mehdi Khan was a criminal. Meer did not agree to the Jehangir Khel's decision and demonstrated his courage when he left the village along with his family. He also showed mercy toward his own brother Mehdi Khan. In Pashtun culture, one is always loyal to his family.

Village Collective Security and Pashtunwali

Pak Kaya village is surrounded by villages where traditional rivalries exist. Sometime these rivalries have had a spillover effect on the village. In the corn harvest season, outlaws roam around in the cornfields. To avoid conflict, the villagers have developed a collective security system. Four men from four households are assigned rotating night duty. During the winter of 1992, there were rivalries between the nearby villages of Hund, Kunda, and Zaida. Pak Kaya village became terrified because of the violent gangs of youths who came to the village and harassed the farmers.

On October 16, a Jirga was called. The Dum, Mohlah Bakhsh, informed all the older men of the village of the Jirga. After the prayer at about 8:pm, they got together at the hujra. Namdar Khan, an old man from the Khabli family, started the discussion by telling the others that the village was really insecure and that they needed to do something. Then, a general discussion took place. A series of proposals were set forth for a collective security arrangement. Each idea was debated. Finally, it was decided that four men should volunteer every night to guard the village. The people were told to be on their guard when the security volunteers blew their whistles. The dependent classes also participated in this volunteer work. No incidents happened, but the village collectively shared the responsibility for security.

In this case study, different tribesmen demonstrated their Pashtunwali. Namdar Khan demonstrated his leadership by sensing the problem and by assembling a Jirga. Each family sent one senior man to attend the Jirga. By participating in the Jirga, each elder demonstrated that he was dutiful and courageous to initiate a mechanism which would provide security to everyone in the village. Each family extended one man to participate in the security guard while the young men had an opportunity to demonstrate their bravery by participating in this guard duty.

APPENDIX B: Salafi Militant Groups Active in the Federally Administered Tribal Areas of Pakistan.

Group	Tribal connection and Location
Abbas Group	Ahmadzai Wazir, South Waziristan Agency
Abdul Rehman Group	Daur, North Waziristan Agency
Angaar Bhittani Group	South Waziristan Agency
Awal Khan Bhittani Group	South Waziristan Agency
Baitullah Mehsud Group	South Waziristan Agency
Bhittani Bhittani Group	South Waziristan Agency
Daur Group	North Waziristan Agency
Dr. Ismael Group	North Waziristan Agency
Ghulam Jan Group	Ahmadzai Wazir, South Waziristan Agency
Gul Bahadar Group	Utmanzai Wazir, North Waziristan Agency
Haji Omar Group	Ahmadzai Wazir, South Waziristan Agency
Haji Sharif Group	Ahmadzai Wazir, South Waziristan Agency
Haleem Group	Daur, North Waziristan Agency
Javed Karmazkhel Wazir Group	South Waziristan Agency
Karawan Naimatullah	Bajaur Agency
Khaliq Haqqani Group	North Waziristan Agency

Group	Tribal connection and Location
Manzoor Group	Daur, North Waziristan Agency
Maulana Abdullah Group	Bajaur Agency
Maulvi Faqir Group (TNSM)	Mamond, Bajaur Agency
Mullah Nazir Group	Ahmadzai Wazir, South Waziristan Agency
Noor Islam Group	Ahmadzai Wazir, South Waziristan Agency
Omer Qandhari Group	Mohmand Agency
Said Alam Mehsud Group	South Waziristan Agency
Saifullah Group	Utmanzai Wazir, North Waziristan Agency
Shah Sahib Group	Mohmand Agency
Shehryar Mehsud Group	South Waziristan Agency
Tehrik-i-Jaish-i-Islami Bajaur	Bajaur Agency
Wahidullah Utmanzai Group	Utmanzai Wazir, North Waziristan Agency

Source: Internal Security Strategy for Pakistan, by Pakistan's Institute of Peace Studies, January 2011.

Bibliography

Agwani, Mohammed. *Islamic Fundamentalism in India.* Twenty-First Century India Society, 1986.

Ahmed, Akbar S. *Millennium and Charisma Among Pathans: A Critical Essay in Social Anthropology,* Routledge & Kegan Paul, 1976.

Ali, Jan A. *Islamic Revivalism Encounters the Modern World: A Study of the Tablīgh Jamā'at.* New Delhi: Sterling Publishers, 2012.

Ayoob, Mohammed. *The many faces of political Islam: religion and politics in the Muslim world.* Ann Arbor: University of Michigan Press, 2007. Retrieved 2009-08-10.

Abun-Nasr, Jamil. *Muslim Communities of Grace: The Sufi Brotherhoods in Islamic Religious Life.* London, Hurst, 2007.

Al-Badawi, Mostafa. *Sufi Sage of Arabia.* Louisville: Fons Vitae, 2005.

Algan, Refik & Camille Adams Helminski, translators, *Rumi's Sun: The Teachings of Shams of Tabriz.* Sandpoint, ID: Morning Light Press, 2008.

Ali-Shah, Omar. *The Rules or Secrets of the Naqshbandi Order,* Tractus Publishers, 1992.

Angha, Nader. "Sufism: A Bridge Between Religions." MTO Shahmaghsoudi Publications, 2002.

Angha, Nader. "Sufism: The Lecture Series". MTO
Shahmaghsoudi Publications, 1997.

Angha, Nader. "Peace." MTO Shahmaghsoudi Publications,
1994.

Aractingi, Jean-Marc and Christian Lochon. *Secrets initiatiques
en Islam et rituels maçonniques-Ismaéliens, Druzes, Alaouites,*
Confréries soufies : éd. L'Harmattan, Paris, 2008.

Arberry, A.J. *Mystical Poems of Rumi, Vols. 1&2.* Chicago:
Univ. Chicago Press, 1991.

Austin, R.W.J. *Sufis of Andalusia,* Gloustershire: Beshara
Publications, 1988.

Azeemi, Khwaja Shamsuddin. *Muraqaba: Art and Science of
Sufi Meditation,* Houston: Plato Publishing,Inc., 2005.

Ballard, Roger. *Desh Pradesh.* C. Hurst & Co., 1994.

Barfield, Thomas. *Afghanistan: A Cultural and Political
History,* Princeton University Press.

Barks, Coleman & John Moyne, translators, *The Drowned Book:
Ecstatic & Earthy Reflections of Bahauddin, the Father of Rumi,*
New York: Harper Collins, 2004.

Bewley, Aisha. *The Darqawi Way.* London: Diwan Press, 1981.

Burckhardt, Titus. *An Introduction to Sufi Doctrine.* Lahore,
1963.

Caroe, Sir Olaf. *The Pathans*: With an Epilogue on Russia, New York: Disney Hyperion Books.

Crews, Robert D. and Amin Tarzi (edited). *The Taliban and the Crisis of Afghanistan*. Harvard University Press, Cambridge, Massachusetts.

Chopra, R. M. "Great Sufi Poets of the Punjab," *Iran Society*, Calcutta, 1999.

Colby, Frederick. *The Subtleties of the Ascension: Lata'if Al-Miraj: Early Mystical Sayings on Muhammad's Heavenly Journey*. City: Fons Vitae, 2006.

Dahlén, Ashk. *Sufi Islam, The World's Religions: Continuities and Transformations*, ed. Peter B. Clarke & Peter Beyer, New York, 2008.

Emin Er, Muhammad. *Laws of the Heart: A Practical Introduction to the Sufi Path*, Shifâ Publishers, 2008.

Emin Er, Muhammad. *The Soul of Islam: Essential Doctrines and Beliefs*, Shifâ Publishers, 2008.

Ernst, Carl. *The Shambhala Guide to Sufism*. HarperOne, 1999.

Fadiman, James and Frager, Robert. *Essential Sufism*. Boulder: Shambhala, 1997.

Farzan, Massud. *The Tale of the Reed Pipe*. New York: Dutton, 1974.

Gowins, Phillip. *Sufism—A Path for Today: The Sovereign Soul.* New Delhi: Readworthy Publications (P) Ltd., 2008.

Haroon, Sana. *Frontier of Faith: Islam in the Indo-Afghan Borderland*, Columbia University Press, New York, ISBN 978-0-231-70013-9.

Idris, Khan. *Jirgas: Pashtun Participatory Governance*, Tribal Analysis Publishing, Richardson, Texas.

Idris, Khan. *Jirgas: The Pashtun Way of Conflict Resolution*, Tribal Analysis Publishing, Richardson, Texas.

Ignatius, David. *Bloodmoney: A Novel of Espionage*, W.W Norton and Company, New York, ISBN 978-0-393-07811-4.

Kepel, Gilles. *The war for Muslim minds: Islam and the West.* Cambridge, Mass.: Belknap Press of Harvard University Press, 2004.

Khan, Hazrat Inayat. "Part VI, Sufism". *The Sufi message, Volume IX—The Unity of Religious Ideals.*

Koc, Dogan, "Gulen's Interpretation of Sufism", *Second International Conference on Islam in the Contemporary World: The Fethullah Gülen Movement in Thought and Practice*, December 2008.

Lewinsohn (ed.). *The Heritage of Sufism, Volume I: Classical Persian Sufism from its Origins to Rumi (700-1300).*

Marty, Martin E. and R. Scott Appleby. *Fundamentalisms Observed*. Chicago: University of Chicago Press, 1994.

Masud, Muhammad Khalid. *Travellers in Faith*. Brill, p. 268, 2000.

Michon, Jean-Louis. *The Autobiography (Fahrasa) of a Moroccan Soufi: Ahmad Ibn 'Ajiba (1747–1809)*. Louisville: Fons Vitae, 1999.

Nurbakhsh, Javad. *"What is Sufism?"* Electronic text derived from *The Path*, Khaniqahi Nimatullahi Publications, London, 2003.

Rabasa, Angel. *The Muslim world after 9/11*. Santa Monica, CA: RAND, 2004.

Roy, Olivier and Antoine Sfeir. *The Columbia World Dictionary of Islamism*. Columbia University Press, p.430, 2007.

Rahimi, Sadeq. "Intimate Exteriority: Sufi Space as Sanctuary for Injured Subjectivities in Turkey." *Journal of Religion and Health*, Vol. 46, No. 3, September 2007; pp. 409–422.

Schimmel, Annemarie. *Mystical Dimensions of Islam*. Chapel Hill: University of North Carolina Press, 1983.

Schmidle, Nicholas. "Pakistan's Sufis Preach Faith and Ecstasy," *Smithsonian Magazine,* December 2008.

Shah, Idries. *The Sufis*. New York: Anchor Books, 1971.

Shah, Sirdar Ikbal Ali. "The General Principles of Sufism," *The Hibbert Journal*, Vol. XX, October 1921/July 1922.

Shaikh Sharfuddin Maneri. *Letters from a Sufi Teacher*. Mountain View, CA: Golden Elixir Press, 2010.

Seker, Nimet. *Jewish and Muslim Mysticism: Jewish Mystics on the Sufi Path.* http://Qantara.de, April 2010.

Wilcox, Lynn. "Women and the Holy Qur'an: a Sufi Perspective." MTO Shahmaghsoudi Publications, 1998.

CPSIA information can be obtained at www.ICGtesting.com
Printed in the USA
LVOW07*0923171215

466978LV00003B/29/P